C000062220

Dadeu

02.2020

# THE
# GROW
## FORWARD MANIFESTO

To Moew;

Enjoy

today

03.2020

HOW TO STEP INTO A PROGRESS MINDSET
TO ACHIEVE A BETTER CAREER AND LIFE

# THE
# GROW
## FORWARD MANIFESTO

"Didem Tekay offers an insightful manifesto for developing a long-term perspective about life, relationships and career, but first and foremost, a long-term perspective about self, about identity. Not just who we are, but who, at the end of the day, we want to be, and what actions we must engage in to become the people in the world that we dream of being. Grow Forward is a user's guide to personal purpose as the driver of personal progress, helping us examine not just the reasons why we should do, but why we should be, and why it urgently matters that we become. It offers clear strategy for leaders to create the best version of themselves—and their teams."
**Whitney Johnson, Author of "Disrupt Yourself"**

## DİDEM TEKAY

Autumn 2019

© 2019 by Didem Tekay
Published by: Redwood Publishing

All rights reserved. No part of this book may be reproduced
or transmitted in any form or by any means, electronic or
mechanical, including photocopying, recording, or by any
information storage and retrieval system, except in the case
of brief quotations embodied in critical articles and reviews,
without prior written permission of the publisher.

Although the author and publisher have made every effort
to ensure the accuracy and completeness of information
contained in this book, we assume no responsibility for
errors, inaccuracies, omissions, or any inconsistency herein.

This book is designed to provide information and motivation to its readers. It is sold with the understanding that the
author and publisher are not engaged to render any type
of psychological, legal, or any other kind of professional
advice. The content of each article is the sole expression and
opinion of its author and is not meant to substitute for any
advice from your healthcare professionals, lawyers, thera-
pists, business advisors/partners, or personal connections.

Design concept and typesetting: HAUS Istanbul
Illustrations: Candan Gürsu


First Printing.

Paperback: 978-1-947341-90-6
e-book: 978-1-947341-91-3

## ACKNOWLEDGMENTS

I have been privileged to find myself in many Grow Circles in my life, with many people. These Grow Circles have consisted of dialogues, heartfelt conversations and sharing in all its forms, from suggestions, to a-ha moments, laughter, silence, joy, mutual discovery, sense-making and learning.

I remember my grandmother wishing for me: 'May the good people surround you and your world'. This wish has carried me through my life, and I have been surrounded with so many good people, all of whom have contributed to my Grow Journey. Around the world they are making a wonderful difference to the people they meet with through their commitment and experiences. Sometimes they are aware of this and sometimes not! Acknowledging them here is an opportunity for me to say, 'Thank you' with my heart.

I start by acknowledging all the thought leaders in this book who contribute to the world through their personal, team and organizational development practices, built on their research, ideas and lived experiences.

I describe MCT, Management Centre Türkiye as the open door to the world for my life. It became a knowledge and development container for me during my career. It connected me with the world's thought leaders, became a bridge for me to connect with the most admired companies and leaders. It challenged me with new ideas, provided fresh ways of thinking and working in teams and organizations.

I want to acknowledge my MCT Partners for their commitment to sustaining our business and keeping the spirit of it alive. Thank you Dr. Alper Utku for your inspiration and capacity to always look ahead; thank you Tanyer Sönmezer for your creative thinking and power of execution. You both shaped a Grow environment for me.

My conversations with John Higgins started the process of writing this book. He supported me to step up, encouraged and helped me to write in English. He brought a clear and compassionate eye to my written pieces.

Whitney Johnson nurtured both me and this book. She offered many helpful insights, became a source of daring, dreaming and doing. Her presence and generosity always reminded me how grateful I am in this world.

Many more people than I can name in many organizations in Turkey and around the globe have provided powerful encouragement for my work. Especially Belgin Boydak formerly of Roche, Demet Akman of Loreal, Emin Fadıllıoğlu of GSK, Feyza Aysan of AstraZeneca, Hakan Alp of Yapı Kredi Bank, Hakan Timur of Sabancı Holding, Pınar Kalay Yemez of Vodafone.

As I have been Growing-Forward in my profession I have attended many workshops and training courses which have given me a mix of both theoretical and practical insights, allowing me to grow in terms of my mindset and skillset. I want to acknowledge two women in particular, Gülsün Zeytinoğlu Ph. D., MCC, CPCC, ORSCC and Dorothy E. Siminovitch, Ph. D., MCC as pioneers who are bringing knowledge and skills to my part of the world. Their presence reminded me of the impact of my presence and how I have an effect on those around me. They showed me how to use myself as an instrument and how to use practical coaching systems in my consulting work, giving me a Grow-Forward experience in my career.

Dr. Sema Özçer brought her compassion and deep listening to our conversations and has become a lifelong mentor for me. She is a dream in a body who reminds to look beyond what I am now.

Mehmet Namık Aydın's creative wisdom and Dr. Alper Tengüz's inspiration provided genuine intellectual companionship, shaped my mindset and gave me a fresh perspective, enabling me to Grow in my practice.

The book itself evolved through teamwork. I want to acknowledge Heather Hunt for her editorial support and bringing her curiosity to the book and Sara Stratton for her spirit and for jumping in and bringing her experience in book publishing. Thank you also to the HAUS istanbul Team for their collaboration and their signature excellence in design.

Özlem Sarıoğlu has been a learning buddy to me in a Group Work, supporting me over the years as both a friend and advisor. Exchanging ideas, feelings and sense-making through our experiences has been and is a Growing-Forward action for me.

Özgün Barış Zaimoğlu is a close friend who has witnessed my Grow starting at my first days in İstanbul. Her open and direct sharing has always provided me with a strong perspective that triggers new cycles of inquiry in me.

My Aunt, who was also my high school English teacher and my early childhood role model, Gönül Atalay has always brought appreciation to my work and my Grow.

My family provided me with an education and my mother Gül Atalay with her strong presence always encouraged me to be a Grow-Forward girl, then woman, in this world. My father and my brother supported me and shaped my relational understanding with the world.

My lifelong partner Koray Tekay with his candor has provided space and companionship during the journey. Our daughter Naz Tekay who still has great contributions to my Grow with her presence deserves very special mention as she is the one who provided me a new role in this world, to be a mother... What a miraculous lifetime Grow-Forward experience!

Thank you...

Didem Tekay, Istanbul 2019

## FOREWORD

Didem Tekay's 'Manifesto' is an invitation to step into the better angels of our nature. She leads the reader through structured, easy to apply, steps for having a better career and life that goes beyond simply acquiring new skills and meeting short term goals set by others.

Full of tips and techniques, she shows how everything rests on the bedrock of our mindset. We have to address who we are and want to be as a person and leader before we can create a meaningful development plan, one that looks back to where we've come from while taking us forward into a better future.

She presents with compelling honesty how she has worked on herself as a person and a leader. She shares what it took to follow the development process she presents.

She takes us inside the experience of engaging with profound professional and personal change, the steps that went as planned and those that on the surface didn't... although it was often those seeming 'failures' that had the deepest impact.

She is one of the very few practitioners who understands that development isn't something you do on your own, but happens through the relationships you are already part of and need to have for your future.

If you are serious about living a better professional and personal life, if you are willing to hear what people really value in you and you value in yourself, if you want to find a life and career that comes from your true heart and will make you a leader of compelling authority... then this is the handbook you've been looking for.

**John Higgins** – Author of 'Speak up. Say what needs to be said and hear what needs to be heard'.

## WRITING TO LEARN AND SHARE INSPIRATION

This is a book about personal and professional growth. It is for anyone who wants to grow beyond the boundaries of how they've been brought up and are expected to be. It's based on my experience and the process I used with myself, and have used with others, to create a better life – at work and more widely.

I started my life as a dutiful daughter in a conservative family rooted in a city on the banks of the Tigris in south-eastern Turkey. Now I'm based in Istanbul and work as a senior business leader with people of all backgrounds and as a respected adviser to many renowned global companies. I'm a lifelong learner who is curiously searching for new insights from all around the world.

To grow as a person is to go beyond what is expected of you. It means noticing and acting on personally felt urges to exceed the limitations of your upbringing. I had always felt stuck in my family, town and even my sense of self. I had an urge to grow that I had to act on.

## My Dream for The Grow-Forward Manifesto

I've been in the professional development business for more than 20 years. I see my company as a pioneering and world class training, facilitation and consulting operation. I joined as a junior client executive and am now the Senior Partner.

I've had the chance to support, work with, and see in action some of the most admired national and international business leaders of our time, as well as engage with inspiring academics and HR professionals.

My intention in writing this book is to form a relationship with you, the reader. I intend to use this relationship I have with you in my mind to help me clarify my thoughts, to learn as I write about how I and others important to me live, love and work in the world. For me, this resonates with the discipline of Action Research which is 'about improving knowledge about existing situations, each of which is unique to the people in the situation, so the knowledge can't be generalized or applied although it can be shared' (Doing and Writing Action Research, McNiff & Whitehead, 2009, pg13). This book shares my unique story, from childhood to the professional leader I now am, taking the unique experience of my Turkish background and culture out into the wider world.

As a life mission, my dream is to share this story and support others who are eager to learn and hungry to grow into a more fulfilling professional and social life. I want to become more aware of my story and how my Grow-Forward path can inspire others, not so they slavishly copy me, but so they feel capable of embracing a greater and richer sense of self in a way that works for them. This book is important to me because of the journey I've been on and the processes I've engaged with. Writing 'The Grow-Forward Manifesto' has given me the chance to look at myself and others reflexively, which means not just noticing my journey but also noticing how I notice my journey. The lenses with which we choose to look at our experience matter as much as the act of examining what our experience has been. Writing this story in this way is a way for me to research how I live my professional and personal life, my practice, and to generate knowledge for me and others.

Working reflexively demands that the researcher be aware of his/her effect on the process and outcomes of research, based on the premise that 'knowledge cannot be separated from the knower' (Steedman, 1991). During my journey, the reflexive turn enabled me to look at myself and ask in all situations: how is this experience part of my Grow-Forward Journey? And as I write this book with this way of thinking in mind, I'm noticing that my story is evolving and I'm searching for what's different and new for me now.

This book has at its heart a very basic question, which we can ask ourselves as human beings.

### *'How can I Grow?'*

From my inquiry I can share what this question evoked in me and where it took me in terms of my development.

Grow is a framework for personal learning and development, that helps people become more fulfilling expressions of themselves in all aspects of their lives. This is done by both close attention to the self and by reaching out to the support and nurturing that can only come from others. It is about you and it's about your relationships with others.

The four distinctive areas of attention that Grow invites people to work on are:

- Growing your sense of self, by tapping into your desire to be better in your life than you ever have been before
- Growing your mindset, the story you tell yourself, or about yourself, to embrace an expanding narrative of who you are and who you're becoming
- Growing your knowledge, abilities and experiences so you can turn your mindset and expanding self-story into real-life action.
- Growing through the actions you take and efforts you make

To avoid too much confusion, I have called it The Grow-Forward Manifesto, so it doesn't get mistaken for the well-established Grow coaching model. In terms of philosophy and practice they could not be more different!

## How the Grow-Forward Manifesto is Different

The Grow-Forward Manifesto invites people to look at their life in the round and reflect deeply on how to live a life that integrates all aspects of what it is to be human, both now and in the emerging future. It does this by:

- Starting with attention to mindset it asks the question, 'Why?' do something, before focusing on the 'How?' of doing it; before asking what skillset you need to develop.
- Establishing a long-term roadmap for your life and career, not just the immediate next step, ensuring that your direction of travel will always be informed by a deeply felt sense of personal purpose.

- Focusing on this internal roadmap and not just the world of short-term external goals
- Combining your life purpose with the expectations of the world around you, such as work and family. How to live better is a social activity, not something that can be known and achieved outside of the relationships you have with others.

I believe there is someone, or some others, in this world who have similar experiences, questions and inquiries as mine. I want to reach out to you and share my story and then I hope to hear from you. I send my story out into the universe and then wait, hungry to hear your experiences so we can continue to grow together. I believe that by sharing my story and hearing from others, I will become more aware of Grow in my life as a leader and how I make choices about developing myself, my team and organization. I also believe that there is something for readers to gain from my story and how it may provoke or encourage them to start an inquiry into their own Grow path.

As a woman leader who lives and works in this part of the world, my intention is also to contribute to overall understanding of Leadership in this region's context. So, I ask myself 'Why Not?' Why not inquire, research, discover, reflect and share with others – value the distinctive insights that come from a part of the world too often overlooked. My hope for this book is to relate with myself and others in common dreams. As you read this book, keep these two takeaways in mind;

- We can all grow beyond what we were brought up to be
- We can all learn from each other's stories

Are you ready to inspire and create your Grow-Forward Journey?

*GROW-Forward Manifesto*

*I can grow and shape a better me in every moment*

*I take accountability to be conscious of
who am I and my impact on others*

*I proactively craft my Grow-Forward plan for the future*

*I value myself and explore every opportunity
to Grow-Forward*

*I value people around me, their insights about
me and I seek their support*

*I value others to listen, share and
Grow-Forward together*

*I feed my curiosity and am alive with
experimentation in this world to Grow-Forward*

*I learn from my failures, I feel the pain and
mobilize my inner willpower*

*I listen to my mind, body and soul to
find the way to Grow-Forward*

*I appreciate my Grow*

CHAPTER ONE

## MY GROW JOURNEY

My story begins in the town in southeast Turkey where I grew up. My family was conservative, middle-class, small (there were just me and my brother) and both my parents worked. My mother was strong, critical and anxious, and advised me, from as young as I can remember, how important it was to be a well-educated working woman, earning my own money.

My father was much more relaxed and outgoing. Less educated than my mother, he spent most of his time travelling to nearby towns for work. He encouraged me to live my life as fully as possible – he was always saying to me: "Remember, we have only one life to live in this world!"

The first time I felt full of excitement and fear at the same time was when my brother was born. This experience of feeling simultaneous and contradictory emotions was new to me! I was both very jealous and filled with compassion towards him! Never before had I felt like this towards the same person. My mother tells me I found my way to deal with this, pretending to be like him, to be like a baby, to get my parents' attention.

As I was five years older than him, I soon started to be given the responsibility to look after him. From the beginning it felt like I was expected to behave more like a mother than a sister towards him.

The town my family lived in was Diyarbakır. Situated on the banks of the River Tigris, it is the administrative capital of the Diyarbakır Province and, with a population of about 1.732.396, is the second largest city in Turkey's Anatolia region. Diyarbakır had a strong political presence with different nations and languages (Armenian, Kurdish, Turkish and Arabic). I grew-up living with different languages in the context of my daily life; Turkish, Kurdish and Arabic were all spoken. The social setting was cohesive and stable, provincial. The political setting, however, was very hectic.

There was a civil war in nearby Syria and on the border with Iraq fighters were also active. There was persistent fear as people went about their day-to-day lives and a general sense of ambiguity, uncertainty about who people were and what was going on. I noticed that these feelings of fear and ambiguity were always with me during my life journey, pushing me to create a reality in which to hide when I found myself in settings that felt like the one I'd grown up in.

As I got older, became a teenager, I had the urge to go beyond the boundaries of my family, my town and myself. I had always felt stuck in that social setting, which despite the political volatility of the regions around it, was too stable, too fixed. I wanted to discover the world, go to new places, meet new people and experience different ways of living.

I'm noticing as I write this that I was searching for a place where I could show my presence freely, from my thoughts to how I expressed myself. I felt squeezed in my hometown. Stifled.

I believed that I had only one choice--to change my context--which meant going to University in another city. My first encounter with the philosophy of social constructionism was experiential; let me describe it. After high school I won exams and entered a well-known University in Istanbul. I was thrown into a vibrant, metropolitan, multi-cultural community. It was a difficult time.

I was now distant from a warm, homey setting and feeling lonely. My sense of self and the world seemed to be under re-construction. I observed others, I replicated how they dressed and found a way to create a relationship with my new social setting which didn't try to copy the one I'd come from. It felt right and I could sense I was progressing beyond boundaries that I'd grown up with, stepping into something new. That progressive energy, and the sense of possibility it gave me, took me into a job after University about which I knew nothing, and which was outside my area of professional education. I'd graduated from the Faculty of Architecture & Urban Planning and the job I took was in training and consulting for a firm that specialized in Retail.

A constant belief remained: I had to be a working woman. Looking at this belief now, I know that I'd acted as my mother had advised me, that I should earn money as soon as possible to set-up my life. There was also my father's encouragement to live the one life I'd been given. The job I was drawn to had its roots in my experience of growing up as a sister/mother supporting my little brother. Wherever I go, I find a way to relate to others by supporting them through my consulting work, being with them and seeing them GROW.

I've now had the experiences of being an employee, manager, leader, coach and consultant over 23 years of professional life. These years have been full of success, learning and progress. Helping others achieve their goals is at the top of my professional, and personal, priorities. I have established, as a guiding principle in my work, my intention to serve individuals, teams, and organizations with all my knowledge and experience.

Throughout my journey with MCT, Management Centre Türkiye, I've gained new experience and knowledge, which has allowed me to change and thrive in my profession and in my larger life. I'm constantly striving to share my experiences with shareholders of the firm and urge the its professionals to do what they can to make MCT a better organization to work in.

I was nominated and listed in 'Forty Over 40's' 2015 list of women leaders and I'm one of the fifty female mentees in the Women on Boards program, an initiative launched to ensure that more women are assigned to top decision-making positions in Turkey's most important corporations.

Stepping back, I see that now it's time for me to share what I've learned in life with others, to be an enabler for their own Grow-forward journey.

I would like to bring my words to a close with a quote from the great poet Rumi, one of the most influential Persian poets of the 13th century:

*Whenever you stop looking*

*Struggle appears*

*Wherever you look*

*Pleasure, drunkenness and rejoicing show their face...*

CHAPTER TWO

## WHAT IS GROW?

Grow is about developing, progressing forward in the sense of self. It's a combination of mindset, skills and actions that lead us to progress in our career, social life and self-world. Grow is about moving forward with balance and momentum as we ride the bicycle of our lives. It gives us the hope and courage to stay on the bicycle even when we feel out of control, the resilience to get back on it when we fall off, as we all do from time to time!

I embrace progress as whatever happens right now is better and more desirable than anything that has happened in the past, so even if I take a stumbling half- step, it's progress.

Let me quote from the Roman Philosopher Lucretius, in Nisbet's book the 'History of Progress'. It reminds me of the process of making progress, how even tiny steps evolve into something transformational.

*'Pedetemtim progredimtes...'*
*'Step by step advancement of mankind over time'*

I believe progress is a delta – it is the difference, the change in a certain quantity of being. In life the quantity always changes, sometimes its money, sometimes its advancement in your career, sometimes it's more about feeling satisfied, successful and happy.

In my own story, the delta of Grow-Forward has three major layers: Mindset, Skillset and Actions. In this book I'll explain the Grow-Forward delta, a formula I believe can be applied at any time, to any area of endeavor you want to make progress in. This is a recipe for everything in your life including, most importantly, growth in your personal relationships.

## The Grow-Forward Mindset, Key Beliefs to Orientate Your Sense of Self

Mindset is the main first layer, the base, the carrier. A mindset is the philosophy, perspective, belief, point of view an individual has on a topic, a situation, or another person. In my professional work as a trainer and consultant, for transformation to take place, a leader or organization needs to undergo a mindset shift. Most of the time, however, people who have responsibility for development ignore the need for mindset development, overlooking the insights of experts such as Carol Dweck who see working on mindset, and especially stepping into a growth mindset (and out of a fixed one), as the key to success in all its forms.

What I've observed in my work fits with a core finding that Carol speaks to in her book 'Mindset' (pg,139), that many leaders do not believe in personal change. As the topics I am asked to work with change over time--from focusing on how to give and receive feedback, inspiring people, creating alignment through storytelling, adopting a coaching leadership style-- the heart of the matter stays the same. Are leader's willing to challenge their own personal point of view? It's the willingness of leaders to change their mindset that is the key to successful outcomes in development and progress.

What can be done to adopt a personal Grow mindset? There are four perspectives, or voices, that you need to hear. What is it that:

*I can do*

*I can shape, design*

*I have the potential for*

*I can have a greater impact on*

As the leader of your own life and a leader in the lives of others, I encourage you to ask yourself these three Grow-Forward Mindset questions:

1. What is the narrative of my life (the story I tell about who I am) and the mindset that I live with which shapes how I approach life?
2. What's the key component of my mindset that keeps me progressing and wanting to Grow-Forward?
3. What needs to shift in my mindset if I am to progress and Grow-Forward?

Pay attention not only to the answers you give to these questions but also to how you go about answering them—i.e. adopt a reflexive habit. In order to develop your mindset, you need to open yourself to other perspectives on life, expose yourself to difference. This means seeking out and experiencing diverse disciplines and cultures, the subjective realities of other lives and imaginations that can be found in literature and biographies and comparing yourself to others through robust and useful benchmarks.

## The Grow-Forward Skillset, Key Skills to Practice

Skillset is the second layer in the Grow-Forward delta, that arc of change. A skillset is the mix of knowledge, abilities and engagement in experiences without which translating Mindset into Action cannot happen. Skillset is in the moment of execution in growing a life. There are the technical skills needed so you can do something about a specific task or situation. Then there are the soft and relational skills, often much harder to acquire and implement. These are the ones that allow us to connect and interact with others, communicate with them in such a way that we feel able to speak up and be heard – and also help others feel safe to speak up and be heard by us.

Ample and compelling research points to how incredibly capable human beings are at learning new skills. Once we're motivated, we have an amazing capacity to learn; for instance we assume that modern communication technology is beyond the reach of the older generation – but tell a Grandparent that they can see their grandchild if they master an iPad and watch the problems melt away! Of course, some skills, especially technical ones, are more easily learnable than others and there are some that will take much time and effort to develop. To Grow you must understand the nature of the skills you need to acquire to support your development. The skills may be at a personal, inter-personal, team or organizational level, or more likely at all of them. To Grow we need to learn how to Grow in the context of the world we are part of or want to become part of.

What can be in a personal Grow-Forward skillset? What are the key skills that equip a person to Grow as a leader in the sense of self? These are the voices of the Grow-Forward skillset:

- The voice of curiosity – are you motivated to be curious about the World around you and your relationship to it?
- The voice of agile learning – are you open to learn in new ways, to embrace other ways of knowing the World and integrating them into your way of being?
- The voice of accountability – do you see yourself as responsible for how you are in the World, as the creator of yourself, and of your relationship to the World?
- The voice of resilience – how do I equip and support myself to be moved but not overwhelmed by the experience of stepping into a new way of being in the world?

With these voices in our heads and as leaders of our lives, I urge and encourage us to ask ourselves these three key

Grow-Forward Skillset questions, with conscious attention to what we notice and how we notice it.

1. What is the key strong skillset that I demonstrate the most?
2. What are the key skills I need to develop right now to reach my goals, to progress, to Grow-Forward?
3. What is needed as a future skill so I can keep progressing and Growing?

The next step to take in grounding the Grow-Forward skillset is to connect into where and how you will go about acquiring this skillset, what will enable your readiness to take action. This requires you to identify what you will undertake in terms of:

- Training – what courses are available for you to attend to acquire technical skills?
- Self-Development Programs – which programs can support you to work on your self awareness?
- Coaching – who can support you to explore your life in the whole?
- Mentoring – who can you be in a relationship with so you can get the guidance and support you need within your professional context?
- Conferences – where can you go to meet and connect with others?

## The Grow-Forward Actions, Key Actions to Take

Once you've done the work on your mindset and skillset, then you need to take those steps that make your Grow-Forward delta live. Without action there is no growth.

At the top of the Grow-Forward delta triangle is the process of being active in the service of your right mindset and skillset.

What can be in a personal Grow-Forward set of actions? What are the key actions that equip a person to Grow as a leader in the sense of self?

Here are the dimensions of the Grow-Forward action set:

- Experimentation – what experiments can test your understanding of the World and how you want to be in it? Experimentation is about acting to learn.
- Hard work – GROW does not happen without effort; you will often have to act against the grain of your established habits, and this will be harder than sticking with how you already know to be.
- Dedication – as the historical cliche puts it, 'Rome wasn't built in a day'. Dedication to the craft of your progress, of Growing into the better you, means paying attention to what you're trying to achieve day after day, month after month, year after year.
- Self-reflection – without self-reflection we can never be sure that we're changing at all. Self reflection and a continuous process of self knowing are essential.
- Sharing – as people we grow in connection with others (as Joyce Fletcher observes). When we see ourselves as isolated individuals, we're less than we could be. Sharing is what we do to be generous with others and to create a climate of generosity, where we all seek to grow together.

With these dimensions in our heads I urge and encourage us to ask ourselves these three key Grow-Forward Action questions, observing what we notice and how we notice it.

1. What are the key actions I'm taking on my own (at my own instigation) to progress, to Grow-Forward?
2. What are the key actions I need to be part of in the company of others, to keep me progressing and Growing?
3. Do I implement my mindset and skillset in the actions I'm taking to progress, Grow-Forward?

Having identified the portfolio of actions you need to instigate and take part in the next step is to be explicit about where and when these actions will take place, what will enable you to step into becoming the better you in terms of:

- Projects – what are the projects I can start or join, at home and at work, that will support my Grow-Forward actions?
- Internships – where can I go to participate in activities that will not otherwise be available to me, given where I am currently working?
- On the Job activities – what can I do in the context of my current work and/or life that will allow me to take Grow-Forward actions?
- Hobbies in action – what are my current hobbies and how can I incorporate new Grow actions into how I perform them? What are the new hobbies I can take up that will make new Grow-Forward actions possible?

## The Grow-Forward Delta Model, Self – Putting It All Together

Set out below is an illustration that shows the Grow-Forward Delta triangle of the self – with the core characteristics that need to take place at each level. Mindset is at the base, on which the Skillset is built before finally being translated into Action that moves you forward.

**Actions**

Sharing        Self Reflection        Hard Work        Experimentation
                                      Dedication

**Skillset**

Resilience        Accountability        Learning        Curiosity
                                        Agility

**Mindset**

i have a              i have the        i can shape        I can do
greater impact        potential         and design

Model 1: Grow-Forward Delta Model Self,
showing three layers of Grow-Forward

Everyone has their own delta; whether it's small or large depends on the mindset, skillset and actions taken. It's always possible to enlarge your Grow-Forward delta through your choices.

Taking time and effort to create the base, the mindset, is the key. Once you make that foundation robust it gets easier to build a skillset and take supporting actions.

## Finding Inspiration to Grow-Forward

I always find it valuable to remember personal heroes and life mentors during my Grow journey. They help me visualize what my Grow-Forward could look like, reminding me of what human beings are capable of, and they give me the energy of inspiration to go on learning and moving forward.

I encourage you to become aware again of the heroes and heroines of your childhood and early years and ask yourself:

- What was the key mindset, skillset and action that made him/her/it your hero or heroine?
- Do you feel any connection with them now?
- What of their mindset, skillset and actions would you like to bring into your Grow-Forward journey?

## Grow-Forward in the Sense of Teams

Most of us belong to groups and teams, at work and in our communities. Grow is something that can also be understood as something that happens as a collective process. Our personal Grow ambition happens as part of our experience of being in teams. In any team there are individual members who are growing and progressing as part of a team that is itself moving forward, progressing as a collective shift.

The relational quality of team members and the leader and their interactions is the key to progress as they interact and make sense of:

- External factors such as regulations, company strategy, competition, changes in business model or stakeholders and,
- Internal factors to do with the team's shared goals, engagement, clarity of roles and responsibilities and trust.

Based on my team coaching and mentoring interventions, individual and team growth happens during the following:

- Defining moments (or critical incidents): All teams have defining moments, when they come face-to-face with decisions or challenges that will set the tone for how the team grows collectively and team members individually. These are the moments when learning can happen, when the quality of dialogue is all important if the team and its members are to progress.
- Living with the need to perform: Teams exist in order to achieve outcomes which are beyond the capacity of individuals alone, and if the team has a meaningful purpose it will feel accountable for its capacity to deliver against outcomes. Achieving results that matter individually, collectively and in the eyes of the world, beyond the team, is an important context in which Grow-Forward can happen.
- Learning through the experience of belonging: Coherent teams experience a natural team life cycle--from individuals, to sub-groups, then to collaboration and finally

to a higher performance mode in which members care about one another. Bruce Tuckman described progress in teams as Forming, Storming, Norming, Performing. This is a perfect definition of a Grow-Forward progress in Teams and needs to be thought about by every team and team leader who wishes to Grow. Many leaders don't understand teams, and most don't act on what they do know. For them there is little opportunity to grow and progress.

- Learning through the experience of sharing: Teams grow through embracing the need to become skilled at collective dialogue and understanding how team success takes place through sharing work approaches and behaviors, and by communicating frequently and clearly.

The mindset of a Grow-Forward team is the voice of the 'High Performing Team' which is an expression of all four points above. It happens in moments of working and being together and in cycles of reflection where the Team steps back to learn together about how it is generating ideas, gathering and organizing information and implementing solutions. The key actions of a team that is keen to grow show up in the habitual practices of group and individual sharing and reflection.

In Virtual teams, the most critical layer is the mindset, as the distance and face-to-face gathering opportunities decline, the purpose and values become more crucial to bond and act on. Assumptions need to be spoken aloud and a robust relationship contract is needed. The grow work for a virtual team and for people new to that context will feel distinctively different than with traditional teams, and for many of them present a challenge as the work is less tangible and often more conceptual.

What can be done to adopt a Team Grow-Forward mindset? There are four perspectives, or voices, that the team needs to hear, focusing on what and how:

*We can do together*

*We can co-create together*

*We are one within our diversity*

*We share a common purpose*

As a leader in a team, ask yourself these three Grow-Forward Mindset questions. As before, pay attention not only to the answers you give but how you go about answering those questions, i.e. adopting a reflexive habit:

1. What is the narrative of my team (the story we tell about who we are) and the mindset which shapes how we approach issues as a team?
2. What's key component of our mindset keeps us progressing and wanting to Grow and be a High Performing Team?
3. What needs to shift in our mindset if we are to progress and Grow?

There is a Team Grow-Forward Skillset, which applies both to the team as a whole and you as a leader in the team. I experience it as voices which prompt me to maintain a Grow focus. They are:

- The voice of collaboration which asks: Are you as a team motivated to collaborate with the World around you and create the relationships you need to be a collaborative force?

- The voice of decision making which asks: Do you have a clear and efficient decision-making process as a team, which has proved to be effective every time?
- The voice of team leadership which asks: Are you able to shift leadership roles and styles within the team to match the needs of the moment?
- The voice of alignment which asks: Is there a commitment to a common understanding of priorities and values? Are you able to own results as a team?

With these voices in our heads I encourage all team leaders to ask themselves these three key Grow-Forward Skillset questions:

1. What is the important skillset that we most demonstrate (as a team) currently?
2. What are the key skills we need to develop right now to reach our team goals, to progress, to Grow?
3. What is needed as a future skill so we can keep progressing and Growing?

In terms of Grow-Forward actions in a team, these are the dimensions of the Grow-Forward action set:

- Constructive conflict - Conflict is an opportunity for discovery, growth and creativity. Healthy conflict occurs when people are giving and receiving feedback with good intent, without falling into the traps of criticism, defensiveness and finger pointing.
- Hard work - Grow does not happen without effort; you will often be having to act against the grain of your established habits, and this will feel harder than sticking with how you already go about things.
- Dedication - Dedication to the craft of your team's prog-

ress, of Growing into a better team, means paying attention to what you as a team are trying to achieve day-after-day, month-after-month, year-after-year.

- Team-Reflection - Team reflection can be seen in action when a team is flexible in addressing opportunities for change and responds positively and creatively to those moments when it can deepen its collective awareness.
- Team Vision- For a team to grow it needs an inspiring shared vision to which all are connected, free of pessimism, hopelessness or hindering memories of the past.

With all this in mind, there are three Grow-Forward Action questions to consider in a reflexive way

1. What are the key actions we are taking as a team to progress, to Grow?
2. What are the key actions we need to take in the company of others, to keep us progressing and Growing?
3. Are we implementing our mindset and skillset in the actions we are taking to progress, to Grow?

## The Grow-Forward Delta Model, Team – Putting It All Together

Set out below is an illustration that shows the Grow-Forward Delta triangle of teams– with the core characteristics of each level. Mindset is at the base, on which the Skillset is built before finally being translated into Action for the team.

Every team has its own delta; whether it's small or large depends on the mindset and skillset it has and the actions it takes.

**Actions**

Team
Vision

Team
Reflection

Hard Work
Dedication

Constructive
Interaction

**Skillset**

Alignment

Team
Leadership

Decision
Making

Collaboration

**Mindset**

We share
common purpose

We are whole
with our diversity

We can co-create
together

We can do

Model 2: Grow-Forward Delta Model
Team, showing three layers of Grow

## Inspiration in Action for a Grow-Forward Team

I always find value in remembering my own personal dream team when on a Team Grow journey. It helps me visualize myself as a Grow Team Leader and gives the energy and inspiration to learn and move forward. I encourage you to be aware of your dream team, a team you were in and where you felt satisfaction and growth. Ask yourself:

- What was the key mindset, skillset and action that made that team a dream team?
- Do you feel any connection with the team you are leading, or are a member of?
- What from then would you like to bring into your team journey?

## Grow-Forward in Organizations and Communities

Grow-Forward in organizations and community is about the culture, taken for granted habits of interaction, about how things are said, who is listened to and what subjects are accepted as discussable. Every organization has a culture which lives in a pattern of relationships and how power is exercised and experienced.

Cultures form, develop and evolve over time. The ways in which things are done--the conventions, rituals and practices--reflect an organization's learning and acquired wisdom. Over time some norms and values may shift or transform, but in the main they are usually very robust. They are passed on to each new generation of people who join, perpetuating the organization's distinctive character.

To make even a half-step toward doing something different in this pattern of interaction is, in my definition, progress, where whatever happens now is better and more desirable than anything that has happened in the past. The interactions within an organization, between the leader (as an embodiment of hierarchical power), and other individuals, and other patterns of relationships are the keys to progress.

In recent decades most organizations have come to understand just how important the health of their culture is to their success. What's more, they're recognizing the need to manage their culture with the same skill and attention they pay to their strategy, their financials, and other key performance measures. Each of us has deeply held beliefs about our organization, our coworkers, our customers, our competitors and our industry. These beliefs and assumptions, and their associated behaviors, determine the culture of an organization. Simply put, "culture is the way things are done around here" (Ouchi and Johnson, 1978).

## What I Observed During My Consulting Interventions;

Organizations need a structure and process to Grow-Forward. They need to:

- **Engage** with a new topic of organizational importance to provoke a response which exposes the normal response of the culture when change is introduced news of difference
- **Discover** the reaction to the topic, paying attention to what the responses really are (not what they're meant to be) as people try to integrate or reject a proposed change

- **Evolve** is the reframing of the response to the topic, bringing to people's attention the spontaneous reaction, and the evolution of a different, better response
- **Deploy** is the act of widening the breadth of the organization exposed to the topic and what has been learnt about the organization's response to date and how that is evolving
- **Establish** is putting in place the necessary structures and supporting processes that will help sustain both the new topic and the evolved organizational response within the dynamics of the culture (which is both established and emerging)

What can be done to adopt a Grow-Forward mindset for an organization? There are four perspectives, or voices, that need to be heard by a high performing organization. What is it that:

*We can do*

*We are committed to*

*We have clarity about in our direction*

*We share as a common purpose*

As a leader of an organization you need to ask yourself these three Grow-Forward Mindset questions in a reflexive way:

1. What is the narrative of my organization (the story we tell about who we are) and the mindset that we live with, which shapes how we work together?
2. What's the key component of our mindset that keeps us progressing and wanting to Grow-Forward and be a High

Performing Organization?

3. What needs to shift in our mindset if we are to progress and Grow-Forward?

In terms of the Organization Grow skillset these are the voices that shape what you need to focus on:

- The voice of coordination – What are you able to work on together as different functions and units of an organization?
- The voice of adaptability – Are you able to adapt to meet changing needs? Are you able to read the world outside of your organization and react well?
- The voice of execution – Are you able to execute plans in a systemic way that explores both the how and what of what needs to be done? Are you able to ensure full accountability for what has been decided, throughout the organization?
- The voice of organizational learning– Are you able to make sense of developments and signals from the world outside of the organization and translate them into opportunities for developing new capabilities?

With all this in mind, there are three Grow-Forward skillset questions to consider in a reflexive way:

1. What is the key skillset that we already most demonstrate (as an organization)?
2. What are the key skills we need to develop right now to reach our organizational goals, to progress, to Grow-Forward?
3. What is needed as a future skill so we can keep progressing and Growing?

These are the dimensions of the Grow-Forward skillset for an organization:

- Outside-in – Grow-Forward is being aware of the external, world and what's happening in other contexts, creating perspective and a sense of possibility. In my consulting work the organizations that struggle most are those that are solely focused on their internal world. To Grow, organizations need to have an 'outside-in' perspective to flourish 'inside-out'.

- Hard work – Grow does not happen without collective effort; you will often be having to act against the grain of your organization's established habits, and this will feel harder than sticking with how you already know to be.

- Dedication – Dedication is a collective act in organizations. Sustaining a commitment to grow will be constantly challenged while achieving short term objectives. The key to success is creating a sense of sustained momentum through small steps that reinfoirce the grow ambition.

- Reflection – Collective reflection and feedback / feed-forward is essential for an organization to grow healthily. It's only through the habit of shared interpretation of experience that people can grow together. Reflection needs to be seen as a social as well as a personal process.

- Dialogue – William Isaacs describes dialogue as 'a conversation with a center, not sides. It lifts us out of polarization and into a common sense and is thereby a means of accessing the intelligence and coordinated power of groups of people' (W. Isaacs: Dialogue and The Art of Thinking Together). If we can create organizational dialogue, people can shift their collective awareness and open a path to grow as an organization.

With all this in mind, there are three Grow-Forward action questions to consider in a reflexive way:

1. What are the key actions we are taking as an organization to progress, to Grow-Forward?
2. What are the key actions we need to be part of in the company of others (competitors), to keep us progressing and Growing?
3. Are we implementing our mindset and skillset in the actions we are taking to progress and Grow-Forward?

## The Grow-Forward Delta Model, Organization
## Putting It All Together

Set out below is an illustration that shows the Grow-Forward Delta triangle of organizations– with the core characteristics of at each level. Mindset is at the base, on which the Skillset is built before finally being translated into Action for the organization. Every organization has its own delta; whether its small or large depends on the mindset and skillset it has and the and actions it takes.

## Inspiration in Action
## Within an Organization and a Community

Take time to remember your own personal best workplaces and/or communities in your Grow-Forward journey. Visualize yourself as a Grow Organization / Community Leader and use this for inspiration to learn and move forward. I encourage you to be aware of your dream of a best workplace.

## Actions

Dialogue      Reflection      Hard Work      Outside In
Dedication

## Skillset

Organizational     Execution     Adaptability     Coordination
Learning

## Mindset

We share     We have clarity     We are     We can do
common purpose     in our direction     committed

**Model 3: Grow-Forward Delta Model
Organization, showing three layers of Grow**

- What was the key mindset, skillset and action that made that organization a great workplace / community?
- Do you feel any connection with the organization / community you are leading, or you are in?
- What are you aware of from then and would like to bring to your organization's / community's journey?

## CHAPTER THREE

## HOW TO CRAFT YOUR GROW-FORWARD PLAN

### What is a Grow-Forward Plan?

In my consultancy work I observe leaders struggling to craft their own Grow-forward roadmap and plan. Many companies have performance systems which connect business outcomes with an individual's development plan and the outcomes for that plan.

Unfortunately, most of the time, these individual development plans are of very poor quality. It starts with the senior Leaders having poorly developed plans, which then cascade throughout the organization from both individual and team perspectives.

Development plans are created, often with little meaningful dialogue between people, and then put away and forgotten. Monitoring doesn't really happen at all.

I need to make an important distinction here between an individual development plan and an individual Grow-forward plan. Development plans are mostly focused on corporate skillsets and feature a one-year horizon. They fit with pre-defined competencies the organization believes to be important and relate to the leadership's expectations for the organization.

In a culture such as Turkey's, which can be described as having a 'high power distance', where those with hierarchical power and authority are treated with respect and deference, development plans rarely focus on mindset development. This context of deference results in basic assumptions about personal development not being challenged.

Most leaders who have grown up in Western influenced cultures, including Turkey, have been encouraged to develop a clear and robust mindset which works well within the parameters of a given world and business context.

However, they struggle when their context changes and they are challenged to shift their mindsets to make sense of the new context. The need to create a Grow-Forward plan, which pays attention to the underlying assumptions taken for granted by an unquestioned mindset.

These assumptions are often underestimated or have not even been considered by many leaders.

Their unexamined mindset leads them to focus on overcoming daily, weekly, quarterly and annual business challenges, and ignore what they need to work on to craft a Grow-Forward plan they can practice.

A Grow-forward plan serves leaders as a road map which they can review on a regular basis to ensure that they are staying on track and making progress in the overall shape of their careers and lives.

The same applies to teams and organizations. We all know that High Performing Teams and Organizations have a vision and clear goals, largely related to the external world. But in my work with teams and organizations I observe that there is very little focus on their long-term progress and their Grow-Forward Plan. The challenge is how to focus on creating a Grow-Forward plan at individual, team and organizational levels.

The Grow-Forward Plan has some defining characteristics. It combines your life purpose with your organization's expectations, if you work in an organizational setting. If you're not part of an organization, it positions achievement of your life purpose in the context of those groups and institutions that you will inevitably have to engage with.

Crafting a Grow-Forward Plan is a process with a holistic approach. You gather all the evidence you have about your past experiences, the feedback you've received, and link this with the future you wish for your life.

As you craft the plan, you'll have the opportunity to reflect and think on your own and with others who are stakeholders in your life. You will build on relationships you already have and building new ones – seeking out those people and groups who can be your allies in your Grow-Forward Journey.

A Grow-Forward Plan is essential for a person to progress. It's about intentionally and consciously choosing a path to follow, not leaving it to chance.

Crafting a Grow-Forward plan is a learnable skill, so I encourage each leader to create their own Grow-Forward plan and guide their teams to do so as well. Before going to the plan structure, I'd like to highlight some mindset reminders.

## The Grow-Forward Plan Mindset, Key Beliefs to Craft a Plan

### Think bold!

To craft a Grow-Forward Plan I encourage you to think boldly in terms of setting learning goals for yourself. This plan is you investing in your future, so take the time to step back and really think big! Visualize the progress you want to see in your life. By visualizing your future, you'll begin to picture something tangible, which can readily be brought to mind, and which should carry within it an emotional charge!

### Stretch yourself!

A good Grow-Forward Plan consists of stretching components. It pushes you out of your comfort zone and presents you with a challenge. If your Grow-Forward plan is too easy, then it's not a Grow-Forward plan. Development is much more than learning. Learning is focused on acquiring new insight or capabilities, which may or may not be applied. Development is focused on making changes in your life that improve personal performance and advance organizational or team objectives.

### Find your 'Unique Presence'

Your unique presence is the key lens you need to see yourself through. Knowing who you are and being willing to create a better version of yourself is a progress mindset.

There are many tools and frameworks available to help you find your uniqueness. Take advantage of the insights that can come from exploring your behavioral preferences and psychometric profiles.

Understanding Self is also about developing an understanding of how you're seen by others, recognizing personal strengths and weaknesses and identifying areas for specific improvement.

Then there is the work we need to do with and about others. We are relational beings and must Grow-Forward in a way that works with and pays attention to others. Other people have different behavioral styles and we need to learn how to read them and respond effectively to their needs and not just our own.

Adapting our style and behavior to connect better and more powerfully with others is an essential developmental action, enriching our range of 'Usable Interpersonal Strategies.'

**Be aware of your 'Learning Style'**

People learn differently, and we all prefer to learn in different ways. Know your learning style! There are lots of tools and frameworks out there to help you discover this! Once you know your style you can craft your plan with learning processes and components that will work for you.

One of the most widely used models comes from the work of Kolb; his model describes Learning as "the process whereby knowledge is created through the transformation of experience. Knowledge results from the combination of grasping and transforming experience" (Kolb 1984: pg:41).

When an individual understands their personal learning style, they can then focus their time and energy on learning experiences that fit their style and needs. As well as being efficient and effective, it can also increase the enjoyment of the learning experience!

## Take accountability for being a Learner

You must take personal responsibility for your Grow-Forward plan; you are the only person who can hold yourself to account for it. You need to be proactive and future focused; the time to focus on development is before it's needed. A positive mindset delivers results and taps into people's natural desire to learn, grow and to be successful in their life and at their work.

As a leader in an organization you need to create a 'Progress Partnership', that is shared between the individual, the manager, and the organization. Development efforts must create value for both the person and the organization for real progress to occur.

## Address your vulnerability

The Grow-Forward process gets you to face personal challenges and acknowledge the gaps you have (and which you'll often have become very skilled at hiding!) Learning and progressing is a challenging process. Make time to reflect and open a space to your vulnerability. Start with what is most important before considering strengths and development areas. Be aware of learning anxiety when you face developing a new skill.

## Create your allies

Who will be the allies you'll need during this Grow-Forward Journey? Ask yourself and list their names. Pay attention to who you are choosing and not choosing. If you can't think of anybody, how can you stretch your choices? Allies are supporters; they also need to have some skills that you need in the process, so make conscious choices regarding who will be enabling your development and progress.

## Grow-Forward Plan Skillset, Key Skills to Craft a Plan

### Crafting

Crafting a Grow-Forward Plan is a systematic, structured way to enable and support people and leaders develop in the best way.

In crafting a development plan use the 70:20:10 Learning and Development Model created by Michael M. Lombardo and Robert W. Eichinger, based on research conducted by the Center for Creative Leadership (CCL). The rule to work with is:

- Seventy percent of learning is experiential. It happens through daily tasks, challenges and practice. Leaders always struggle to define experiential on the job micro tasks to facilitate learning. They think grow and development are individual and isolated activities. In fact, they are not. Experiential learning happens in moments of everyday interaction with people. Plan those interaction moments intentionally and consciously to create a play area for your growth. This may be a team meeting or a meeting with a conflicting peer or your boss. How you choose to be is your proactive action.

- Twenty percent of learning is social. It happens with other people, and through such practices as coaching and mentoring. Social learning mainly occurs in reflection with others. A mentor, ally, coach or learning buddy provides opportunities to bring up a development topic and reflect on it. Powerful introspection in the company of others is the key to grow forward.

- Ten percent of learning is formal. It happens through structured face-to-face or online training courses and programs designed to develop a skill. Most programs provided by companies or open training and development programs aim to fit in this category. With advances in technology and mobiles, digital learning is disrupting traditional in-class learning. Learning anytime, anywhere is the future of learning.

## Executing

Executing a Grow-Forward Plan starts with focusing on relevant priorities for the near future. It is followed with implementing something every day and reflecting on 'What Happens.' Seeking support, getting feedback and feedforward (in the sense of people's responses to proposed actions), while monitoring progress makes execution a reflective learning process and not simply a static process of ticking off tasks completed.

In execution there are two selves, one who is executing the Grow-Forward Plan, the other who is reflecting on the process and being coach to the other self. Your personal engagement in the execution process determines the quality of the outcomes.

## Feedback / Feedforward

Receiving feedback/feedforward is a vital source of insight. They are critical to performance improvement both in terms of actual outcomes and the process with which outcomes were achieved. Yet they can be difficult to get and give – in cultures which focus on short term performance plans, learning and long-term development too often are viewed through the lens of immediate advantage only.

Once you have crafted and started to execute your Grow-Forward Plan, seek feedback from people about how they experience what you have achieved and the impact they see, and engage in dialogue with people around feedforward – that focuses on the future. These feedback/feedforward relationships will be an essential context for creating a developmental Grow network around you.

**Agility**

Agility is a key skill in executing a Grow-Forward Plan; without it there is no opportunity for continuous learning, for enriching and growing your Grow-Forward plan relative to others and in emerging contexts.

By keeping your mind open so you can embrace the agility needed to gain new insights, modify the plan and adapt the plan to changing needs. Examining past failures and learning to plug and play with new learnings and skills will enable you to be agile in your Grow-Forward Journey.

## Grow-Forward Plan Actions, Key Actions to Take

**Visibility**

Make your Grow-Forward plan visible to yourself and others. Find a way that works for you to keep your Grow plan in mind, such as keeping a drawing with you that speaks to your plan and to where you are with it.

Some of you may want to put in place a series of dates in your diary that reminds you to take time out to look at your plan. The more you are constantly reminded of your Grow-Forward plan the more you will keep it in mind as you go about the day-to-day of your life and work. Creating a conversation about your plan with colleagues also creates a social contract, a sense of social expectation in your relationships with others. It helps cement your commitment to progress in your life and grows that perception and expectation in those around you. It will also enable you to find allies and get insights on your plan.

## Reflecting

Reflecting on progress is an essential discipline. Without reflection plans and progress become fixed and trapped into unconscious, rather than chosen momentum. Busyness takes precedent over meaningful growth.

Reflection has both an inner and outer arc. It's the internal process of self-inquiry of engaging with your subjective reality and the external one, of inquiring into the context of the impact you've had on the world around you.

There are many forms of reflecting, but one of the most important is the habit of journaling, which allows you to have a record of how your plan is happening over time – it gives you a source of in-the-moment data for you to refer to, noticing patterns and habits which might otherwise escape you.

## Sharing

A Grow-Forward process is a relational and generous activity. It's about stepping beyond those boundaries that you have known and being with others in ways that will serve you well now and in the future. It's about growth in connection (as Joyce Fletcher puts it).

Sharing your learnings is a key action to deepen your learning and progress and provides evidence of a generous growth mindset. Share critical moments, experiences, insights, glimpses of awareness, times when you have fallen short (people will grow in their connection to you if they experience your falling short as well as your triumphs).

## How to Be a Grow-Forward Catalyst in Your Relationships

We are always in relationships with others when we are working and living. As humans we are inherently social animals defined as much by the 'we' of our relationships as the 'I' of our individual identity. It's important to learn key concepts, skills and tools to be more effective in our relationships with others. Being in relationships well is not something that happens by accident; it's an ability that can be learned and always improved upon, something we can grow.

Relationships are always part of wider systems. Whatever we do and whoever we do it with has an impact on the wider ecology of which we are part. However slight it might feel, we are always part of a bigger picture which we can influence.

If we're conscious enough and have the courage to intentionally grow ourselves, it will have an effect on the relationships we are in, and the world we relate to and act in. How you relate with others and with the world is a good indicator of your personal progress and where you are on your grow journey.

The whole world and the life you live in your relationships with others provides you with many grow opportunities, and the capacity to see how your new way of being has an impact, not only on you, but in the world in which you live.

## Your Grow-Forward Dialogue in Relating with the World

Part of the process for growing the quality of your dialogue with the world comes from working with different ways of experiencing and expressing what is going on for you.

In the following pages I explore the importance of Poetry, Photography and Art to me and my grow journey.

### Poetry

Poetry was always, and remains, a corner stone in my grow journey. I always try to find poems that communicate with the deepest parts of my being, that get me in touch with the heart and the head, those things that I feel and think deeply about. It's like exploring a new being in me, and it surprises me how the writer could have had such similar experiences or feelings as I have.

Over the years, I've discovered that poems are also a way of connecting me with others. I remember my mother's very small and old poetry notebook from my early childhood and how it connects me with her. With my very close friends I share the poems that describe my moods and desires and in return I get poems from them; this creates a deep intimacy between us which evolves and deepens our relationships and allows us to grow together. Poems help us to know each other and to build a community of felt connection. I also gain knowledge about different histories, writers, languages and emotions that connect them, and now me, with the world. Poems inspire me; they speak to the universal and are bridges that connect worlds. A well-crafted phrase in a poem can open our eyes and our hearts as nothing else, helping us see even the most ordinary experiences in an entirely new way.

In our relationships with the world, we shape and are shaped by poetry and so become open for the next stage of our journey – and this is the progress of grow.

David Whyte's poem 'Working Together' is a great description of this progress:

### Working Together

*We shape our self to fit this world*
*and by the world are shaped again.*

*The visible and the invisible working together*
*in common cause, to produce the miraculous.*

*I am thinking of the way the intangible air passed at speed*
*round a shaped wing easily holds our weight.*

*So, may we, in this life trust to those elements*
*we have yet to see or imagine, and look*
*for the true shape of our own self, by forming it*
*well to the great intangibles about us.*

*— David Whyte*
*from The House of Belonging (©1996 Many Rivers Press)*

## Photography

Photography has exploded into our world in the last decade or so and is now an ordinary part of how we all practice dialogue. With smart phones and social media everybody is a photographer nowadays.

I use photography as a dialogue tool in my workshops. What we notice in a photograph, and what it evokes in us, is a way of deepening our awareness and progress. Whenever I go to a museum, I look for photos that inspire me, that grab my attention

Stephen ESPO Powers, focusing on the language of signs,
typography, culture, 2019

and connect me with my inner world. I leave that photo with a new discovery and learning. I'm always a step forward from who I was before I looked at it. I discovered that I can hardly describe 'Beauty' with words, but I can easily describe 'Beauty' with photos. Photography is an essential part of my practice of dialogue, helping me to explore new ways of thinking and expressing insights I don't have the words for.

Below, the first photo is from the San Francisco Museum Of Modern Art, SFMOMA. It's a picture reminding me that 'I'm My File' and inspires me to write my story. It reminds me to capture details of my daily routine. When I look at this photo I see Grow-Forward; the ladder to raise up and support others as well as providing support for myself.

The second photo taken by me at a London café in Bloomsbury, is a reminder of excellence and dedication for me, and a warm smile. It inspires me to learn a new skill, how to make great craft in a cup of coffee.

## Art

Art is a very powerful voice for me when it comes to Grow-forward. Its diversity of form, how it exists in visual, auditory or performing artifacts, expressing the author's imagination, their conceptual ideas, their technical skill – these always speak to Grow for me and how it can take so many forms.

Whenever I feel myself to be stuck, not progressing to the vision of my new context or the new version of me, I feed myself with art. Museums, street artists, graffiti – all can show me a path, all can inspire my creativity. With art in my heart I go, see and create new inquiries for myself and for those around me. Sometimes I find myself remembering an interior of a museum or gallery and designing the workshop room accordingly. It's not only about seeing an artifact or setting, but it's also about moving it to another form. Art and Grow mix things together to bring about the new.

I want to share a principle from my early profession of architecture: Form follows Function. It's associated with late 19th and early 20th century architecture and industrial design in general. It means the shape of a building or object should primarily relate to its intended function or purpose.

I see similarities in an individual's, team and organization's grow forward manifesto. In "Form follows function" a formal analysis of a work of art describes how the elements and principles of a particular artwork come together, independent of their meaning and the feelings or thoughts they may evoke in the viewer.

You have a vision for the state you want to be in, the function of the vision is its context. The form is you and how to grow and take shape according to that function/context. If I could symbolize it with a piece of art, imagine working a piece of clay with your hands. It's you, working on you, and giving a form for a forward state, the context (the function) you want.

## A Grow-Forward Recipe

James Clear talks to the power of tiny gains to be better every day in his book Atomic Habits. The effects of small habits compound over time. If you can get just one percent better each day, you'll end up with results that are nearly 37 times better after one year.

### 1% BETTER EVERY DAY

1% worse every day for one year.  $0.99^{365}=00.03$
1% better every day for one year.  $1.01^{365}=37.38$

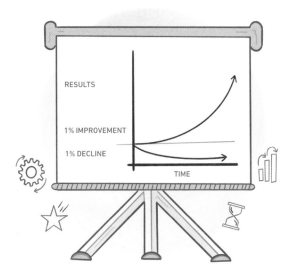

RESULTS

1% IMPROVEMENT

1% DECLINE

TIME

**Model 3: Grow-Forward Delta Model**
**Organization, showing three layers of Grow**

Smaller but consistent tasks and tiny changes bring about faster grow results. Small habits and little choices are transforming us every day. Whether it's a step, or 10 steps, you are moving forward and progressing intentionally and consciously. I love an anonymous quote which speaks to the decline of our grow--when we allow laziness to take hold, there are consequences because "time always gets its revenge."

## Appreciation of Learning and Grow

In the Grow-forward Delta Model, the base of the pyramid is mindset. The Grow-forward mindset appreciates learning and change. For me, Eric Berne's work on Transactional Analytics was an important learning and point of departure in my grow mindset.

Transactional Analysis is a technique that investigate human relationships by focusing on the precise content of people's interactions and what stood out most for me was the idea that when people are interacting, they are giving and receiving strokes. Strokes can be positive or negative because any transaction that acknowledges another person is a stroke no matter how it feels. Positive strokes have significant results in driving positivity and feed willpower and motivation to move forward. Most of the time we move forward with tiny changes and learnings but don't allow ourselves to appreciate it and experience a positive stroke. It's the same with those around us, when we don't appreciate what we see in them and don't give them a positive stroke either. We need to become more conscious of these small moves forward, notice how we and those around us grow, and give out positive strokes – it doesn't matter of they are verbal or non-verbal, they'll make a difference! In my team workshops I try to make sure I end with an appreciation session, with people giving positive strokes to one another based on how they've experienced each other. I see the positive impact in people's faces, some of whom are otherwise too shy to receive such feedback. I see others who struggle with giving positive strokes to someone else, trying to find the right words.

Claude Steiner in his book 'Emotional Literacy' opens a new perspective into how to be intelligent with our hearts in our relationships. Mostly we think that when we appreciate or give positive strokes, we lose power and control. In his work, Steiner shows how our positive emotions actually work for us.

With a Grow-forward perspective we need to be aware of our mindset towards our grow and the grow of others. To anchor this awareness, I'd recommend as an annual ritual that you look at your last year and try to define and describe grow for you over that time. What went very well? Where do you feel you can see Grow-forward happening in your career and life? List the people, teams or community that were in your service in this Grow path? Then review your inner emotions and define a way to appreciate their contribution to your Grow-forward. Give them and yourself a stroke in your own way.

## Crafting a Grow-Forward Plan in 7 Steps

Making a Grow-Forward Plan requires a holistic approach which I'll summarize in this section. Most successful executives are the ones who not only invest time to think but also create a plan to gather, focus and execute their thoughts. You are accountable for your grow, so you are accountable to create your Grow-Forward plan.

# Crafting a Grow-forward Plan in 7 Steps

What do you know about yourself?
Review and List

What is possible for you in the future?
Dream and Visualize

What is your Grow-Forward Focus?
Write it Down and Make it Visible!

What is your Grow-forward Plan?
Execute and Monitor It

Who are your allies?
Share and Evolve Your Progress

Where are you in Your Grow-Forward Plan?
Sit Back and Reflect

How will you appreciate your own Grow-Forward progress?
Appreciation and Celebration

## Step 1
## What Do You Know About Yourself?
## Review and List

This step is intended to connect your internal self-awareness as well as your external self-awareness. Your inner self-awareness shows how aware you are of your values, passions, aspirations and habitual responses. Your external self-awareness shows how aware you are of how others see you and experience your impact on them. Here is a checklist for you to use:

√ Look at your performance feedbacks

√ Review your 180, or 360, degree feedback

√ Review your personal preferences and psychometric profiles

√ Ask for feedback from people who work, interact or live with you

√ Review defining moments (a context change, success, failure, loss, gain...) in your life, career or past

√ Look at your childhood hero, what were the qualities of that person that made him/her a hero or heroine?

√ Look at the patterns in all these resources and ask: Are there meaningful patterns? List them.

*Ask 'what' questions of yourself:*
What are the key strengths I show most often?
What are the situations I struggle in?
What skills do I need to demonstrate more?
What's my learning style?
What do I need do to make sure I'm in the best situation to learn?
What's my impact on others?

## Step 2
## What is Possible for You in the Future?
## Dream and Visualize

Grow-forward asks you to think about the possibilities that could serve you in the future to become your future self. The actions you take may be large or small, but as you take them you need to always keep in mind your current and future mindset. Taking the time really to think about and imagine your future may not be easy - and because it's never urgent (only important!) we tend to postpone it or put it off when something comes along to distract you.  It's crucial you force yourself to get out of your comfort zone of busyness and immediate priorities and think about yourself strategically. Here's a checklist you can use to help dream and visualize the future you:

- √  List the goals that you want to achieve in your career and life.
- √  Look at the big picture of your whole context (work, family, community, friends...) and make a quick assessment. What are the things you are happy with? In which part do you want to progress?
- √  Think about your context. What are the things that support you to be your best in this context? List them.
- √  Foresee the short-term changes in your context - what will evolve and how do you see yourself in that changing world? List the possibilities of this new context for you.
- √  Anticipate the long-term changes in your context - what might evolve and how do you see yourself in different future scenarios? List the possibilities of possible new contexts for you.
- √  Review your skills - are there any skills you are not using but you can use in the near future in a new context? List these skills.

√ Think about the mindset that's going to be needed in the near future for your growth.

*Ask yourself these 'how' questions:*
How is your external reputation seen?
How might the context of your life evolve and how do you dream yourself into that context?

## Step 3
## What is Your Grow-Forward Focus?
## Write It Down and Make It Visible!

Steps 1 and 2 provide a range of possibilities for you and your future. The Grow-forward plan gives you a focus to this range of possibilities. With Step 3, it's time for you to focus on your key assets and the points of progress you want to see. Part of what gives this Step focus is the discipline of making these points visible by writing them down, establishing a constant reminder of what you are seeking to become and achieve.

Here's a checklist you can use to give your written plan focus and visibility:

√ List your context's top five characteristics in terms of values, drivers and the key skills that get rewarded (if you are working for a company, you can use the leadership expectations the company has for future leaders).
√ Write your dream for your future state.
√ Write your Grow-forward mindset statement.
√ List your top 3 key strengths in terms of skills.
√ List you top 3 key progress areas in terms of skills.
√ List your top 3 actions to progress in these skill areas.
√ Draw your Grow-forward Delta Model and make it visible on your smart devices and other personal spaces.

*Ask 'why' questions to yourself:*
Why are my top strengths critical for the near future?
Why is my Grow-forward Delta Model relevant for me and for others?

## Step 4
## What is Your Grow-forward Plan?
## Execute and Monitor It

You are ready to use your learning style to choose and deepen your actions, tasks and activities for your key progress areas. While choosing your relevant actions you need to keep in mind that for Grow, progress is not going to be the same experience for you for every skill or progress area. For some you'll need to practice more and allow more time. It's crucial for you to seek out and find opportunities to try new skills and to overcome the anxiety that comes when learning something new (especially when you're used to being excellent in your established skill set). Grow is the same as doing daily exercises for a healthy body; learning everyday makes you have a fit and healthy mindset and skillset. Here's a checklist you can use to execute and monitor the progress of your plan:

√ Look at the summary you created in step 3. What is the essence of this focus? Try to think and give a name to this focus.

√ Remember the 70 - 20 - 10 principle in crafting a plan.

√ For each strength and progress area write down your Grow activities. Write down how 70% of progress will come from daily tasks, challenges and practice, 20% through other people, such as coaching and mentoring and 10% through structured training courses and programs.

√ List other activities that can support your learning and grow such as art, hobbies, other interests, or different disciplines...

√ Document the specific activities you need to participate in and establish a timeline that reflects the learning and progress you're committing to.

√ List anything you'll stop doing – and by when.

√ Explore different types of learning formats and experiences to find what works best for you.

*Ask 'what if' questions of yourself:*
What if I do all activities and grow?
What if I postpone and/or fail to execute my plan?
What if I need more time to digest and progress?
What if I progress exponentially i.e. much faster than I expect?

## Step 5
## Who are Your Allies?
## Share and Evolve Your Progress

Once you have your plan ready, share it with colleagues, friends and thinking partners. Get their insights. Getting others involved always improves a plan. Although it may seem only relevant to you, you'll be doing the work to progress in relationship with others. Ask for real time feedback and try to bring your curiosity when receiving it – seek to understand rather than explain or defend.

Having allies has always worked for me. After many years of my career I've become aware that in every important decision I need to hear from a wide group of people. They're the ones who

I can share ideas with, get different perspectives and feedback/ feedforward from on what I need to do. Here is a checklist for ensuring you share and evolve your plan:

- √ Make a list of people in your life and map out how you can get support from them
- √ These people could be a coach, a therapist, a thinking partner, a colleague, a peer, a friend. Know who your allies are.
- √ Hold a dialogue with them, explaining your intention to get their commitment. Make a relational contract with them to create a safe and trusted space for you both to communicate.
- √ Plan your interaction type and timing.
- √ Identify a learning buddy with whom you can share your new learning and exchange ideas on progress topics.
- √ Notice insights, take time to digest them, think, reflect and then build your own narrative before acting on it.
- √ Appreciate people's contribution to your progress and give feedback to them regarding their roles and its impact on you (they might also want to share feedback on your impact on them).

*Ask 'who' questions of yourself:*
Who can be with me in my Grow-forward journey?
Who is the best learning buddy for me and who can benefit from my learning and sharing?

## Step 6
## Where Are You in Your Grow-Forward Plan?
## Sit Back and Reflect

I always remind myself (and other leaders who are fans of action) of Peter Drucker's advice: 'Follow effective action with quiet reflection. From the quiet reflection, will come even more effective action.' Leaders in my coaching and consulting work mostly avoid reflection; they are addicted to action. Little work has been done on how to develop reflective habits in such people.

Journaling in all its forms is a great tool for establishing careful thought and reflection. Whether people do it through a daily or weekly written diary, or through voice messages to the self, or through Art, Poetry and Photography, journaling provides the evidence for what is going on for a person and an audit-trail of their commitment to grow.

The Grow-forward plan covers a period of up to 18 months according to the specific needs of an individual. Within the plan there need to be explicit times set aside for stepping back in a deliberate fashion to reflect on where you are now with your plan and where you are heading.

A Grow-forward plan evolves over time and changes in response to circumstances. It's not a static thing, done the one-time and set in concrete. You should expect your plan to change after your reflections, with some new actions needing to be integrated into it. Here is a checklist for stepping back and reflecting:

- √ Create a journal for your Grow-forward plan and personalize it as a tool for your development.
- √ Explore how to reflect and ask the right questions.
- √ Set aside times to reflect and make them part of your Grow-forward plan.
- √ Take a time out and step back to reflect if you experience something significant in your life - or find yourself describing a moment as transformative.

√ Use journaling at transformative times. Describe the event, your emotions at the time and the actions that arose.

√ Read your journal at least weekly and pay attention to the patterns. Is there something that needs to be given more attention and acted upon?

√ Incorporate your reflections in your Grow-forward plan. Update it where and when needed.

*Ask 'where' questions of yourself:*
Where am I in my Grow-forward journey?
Where am I heading to?
Where does my learning need to be boosted?

## Step 7
## How Will You Appreciate Your Own
## Grow-Forward Progress?
## Appreciation and Celebration

Appreciating your own grow and the grow of others is a Grow-Forward Mindset attribute. You always need to focus on getting better at every moment. There will always be some obstacles in your Grow way, some barriers that you never thought of before. Like riding a bicycle, you need to keep going, whether you're traveling fast or slow.

Appreciation comes in every moment that you recognize you've made progress, within yourself, and in the impact you're having on others. Involve others in your appreciation and celebrate your Grow. Feel the power of pride. Here is a checklist for appreciation and celebration:

√ Explore how to give and receive appreciation.

√ Set aside times for appreciation. Put milestones in your Grow-forward plan.

√ Appreciate yourself in your own unique way. For some people this is a glass of wine, for others it's buying a new journal. Some people simply like saying good things about themselves to the mirror. The choice is yours!

√ Use journaling to record what you're appreciating about where you've come to and where you're going in your life. Write down your emotions and the impact of Grow in your life.

√ Show appreciation to your allies and supporters. Share your thoughts and emotions with them.

√ Celebrate your progress in your own way.

√ Put a new Grow-forward goal in place for the next celebration.

*Ask 'how' questions to yourself:*

How was the Grow-forward journey?

How do I feel now?

## Actions

Sharing

Self Reflection

Hard Work
Dedication

Experimentation

## Skillset

Resilience

Accountability

Learning
Agility

Curiosity

## Mindset

I have a
greater impact

I have the
potential

I can shape
and design

I can do

Model 1: Grow-Forward Delta Model Self,
showing three layers of Grow-Forward

CHAPTER FOUR

## THE GROW-FORWARD IN THE SENSE OF SELF

In this chapter I use my own experience to illustrate developing a Grow-Forward plan. I share some personal truths I had to work with and the things I did to bring Grow to life. I've deliberately utilized my personal experience in some detail – because I wanted to give you a real sense of the sorts of activities and challenges that I went through. I've also shared some of the real time responses I've had in order to show how subjective and personal a Grow plan process is – I didn't want to give you a polished, easy to read, representation of what I've been through (and am going through), or leave you with a sense that this is something you can do without commitment. I also wanted to demonstrate its iterative nature; a Grow plan is not a simple linear process – and sometimes you'll want to get somewhere before you're ready.

### My Grow Story Having the Courage to Look in the Mirror

From Gergen's perspective, all human intelligibility (including claims to knowledge) are generated within relationships.

It's from relationships that humans derive their conceptions of what is real, rational, and good – reality is in these terms a "social construct" not something that exists outside of the human context or how people frame what they see. When I look to my family and the world I grew up in, I see that I formed a series of beliefs about how to be in relationships with others, and what made certain things true. How I responded to others and they responded to me shaped who I was, gave me a language for talking about and knowing the world. When my social setting changed, I found myself evolving with the others around me; by adapting to the new setting I found a new way to shape and know myself and the world around me.

At this point, my personal behavior preferences also gave me clues regarding how I see the world and relate with others. I remember my father calling me 'yabani', in Turkish, to describe how he saw me relate with others. It translates into English to mean words to the effect of: 'clumsy (or crude/blunt)', 'shy to speak', 'different'. I experienced myself at that time not so much as being 'shy', as being angry. Over time I have deepened my understanding of my personality. The breakdown of my personality traits were provided to me as a personal profile in a workplace report. I share it here as an example of the type of feedback that can be very useful when beginning your Grow work. As you can imagine as you read this, some of the things that were said were easier to hear than others!

## The External Persepctive:
## An Insights Discovery Report

Insights has been brought to life over 20 years ago by Co-Founders (and father and son) Andi and Andy Lothian. Insights with its network help people understand themselves better as individuals and leaders. Insights Discovery is a psychometric tool based on the psychology of Carl Jung, it is built to help people understand themselves, understand others, and make the most of the relationships that affect them in the workplace. In this chapter you'll read my Insights Discovery Personal Profile which I use to increase my awareness about me and list my strengths as well as my possible weaknesses.

Didem is concerned about the welfare of others and can feel compelled to do something tangible to help. She is careful and considerate in the decisions and actions she takes, to ensure she will make a positive impact. She values her care-giving role and the responsibility that comes with it. She can get a great sense of self-worth by being able to do something that makes a real difference. Didem may worry that her goodwill and offers of kindness are not utilized. She can take it personally and get upset if she is criticized or if something does not go to plan.

She tends to keep precise records and can be a great source of reliable information. She needs to be anchored to reality and well grounded, in order to feel comfortable facing challenges. Didem is able to recall information accurately, which allows her to organize and categorize past events. She has the gift of remembering lessons from history, which she can draw on when needed.

Didem's tendency to go over the same things in the same way over and over again can become tedious to others. She can be overly intent on keeping things the way they have always been. She's motivated by her gift of caring for others and appreciates the trust that others put in her. She has the ability to recall details and looks to use this information as a source of help for others.

Didem looks to her personal experience and wisdom to find the solutions that will benefit others. She relies on the foundation of her experience to come up with answers to current problems. Didem may become blinkered by looking solely into her own knowledge and experience for all the answers and may miss other key factors. She can recall and mull over past hurts for a long period of time, finding it difficult to let them go.

Didem can be seen as the disciplined arm of authority and protector of order. She likes to be in the thick of things, taking direct control of the situation or task. Typically, she directs her efforts towards planning, organizing, and completing a task. She wants to impact the external world with her logic, introducing a plan of action to move things forward. Didem may stifle a great initiative by trying to over-control and organize the process. At times, Didem can come across as an aggressor, needing to do it all herself and keeping total control. Her natural balance of caring and protection may make her a source of great comfort to others. Even though she may have a gentle nature, she also has ability to be forthright and challenging, especially when she thinks that others are being threatened. Didem is a caregiver and a guide, providing both nourishment and direction to others. She is encouraging and supportive while at the same time being very protective of anyone in her care.

Being a highly creative person, she will feel compelled to take note of her intuitive flashes of brilliance and record them in some way. She is comfortable with the prospect of just setting off on a journey and finding her way as she goes. Didem likes to set a course for others to follow, even when she is not sure where it is ultimately heading. She has the ability to anticipate problems, sometimes even before they are seen or articulated. In her efforts to present tangible solutions, her daydreaming can distract her from the process.

## The Internal Response Making Sense of the Report

I can see how I had created reality and how it shaped how I relate to the world. I can see what I believed and how those beliefs made me behave in the way described in the report. And I can hear my inner voice telling me my reality about how I am in my relationships with others and with myself which shaped my mindset:

*'Be polite and look for the needs in others so you can support them...*

*Don't have too many friends; have a few trusted ones you can be close to and keep your distance from others to protect yourself from them'*

*'There are times you need to show your presence and times not to show up, be aware of when these times are and don't make any mistakes by showing up when you're not wanted or not being there when people want you'*

*'Have a balance of give and take in your relationships, always support others, first give and wait to take from the other... There should be a mutual benefit in each relationship, think function-ally, if someone is not giving to you in a way that helps you prog-ress yourself or your situation do not lose time... take steps to get what you need...* **If the other in the relationship makes any action which disregards your contribution to him/her, do not stay in that relationship, it's all over'**

*'There is always a way in a relationship'*

I now know when and where I shaped these realities. I can also see that there is a defining moment, a story behind each statement. These statements give me pain and bring into sharp focus what other choices of relating might be possible.

## Supporting Others and Showing Presence As a Way of Relating with Others

My story took me to a place where I noticed my frames of relating with others, the need for mutual benefit, trust, politeness and a balance of give and take. Describing a journey is always exciting for me, because you reflect on what you have experienced, and become aware of many things that you didn't notice at the time.

When I look back at my journals, the books and articles I've read (and the notes I made on them), the workshops I've run and participated in, action learning sets I've been part of and those all-important, in-the-moment discussions and conversations, I can see the learning and reflection I've been part of.

Bringing all these experiences to my conscious attention, I notice that there's a change I can see in them that I want to deepen. I've been thinking of this in terms of my 'case' since I heard the simple question: 'What is "Your Case" that you want to explore' in my Masters' thesis process. The 'Case' demonstrates something I want to develop and work in order to progress. I realized that it may seem a simple question, but for me it was very hard to answer. When I heard the word 'Case' I saw themes coming to the surface of my conscious thought, two in particular: **Supporting Others** and **Presence**. Supporting others is a way of building and maintaining a relationship. Presence is a way of expressing and using my sense of self.

According to Mary Tolbert and Jonno Hanafin (Use of self in OD consulting: What matters is presence, p72), presence represents the translation of personal appearance, manners, values, knowledge, reputation, and other characteristics into interest and impact. Presence is not manufactured. Everyone possesses Presence, regardless of the level of awareness of the impact of that presence. For me Presence is use of self with intent and I know that there are times my intention is to avoid showing up with too much Presence.

I started to think and reflect on 'How am I in supporting others and showing presence?' In my inner discussions it seemed these themes were relevant to me.

## Learning About Presence in a Way that Fits with My Learning Style

I'm best at understanding a wide range of information and putting it into concise, logical form. I need time to reflect before passing this information on to others. I also need a wide range of information that comes in many forms and from many sources. This takes time and prevents me showing my presence much of the time.

I often hear people say: 'Didem, I see you're being silent; why don't you say anything?'

Meanwhile, I see myself thinking and watching, bringing my knowledge and past experiences to the group when I'm ready, to support others. I'm observing the group, watching participants, listening to their dialogue and seeing themes and patterns. Then the time will come when I'm ready to share what I see.

Then I also found a clue for my avoiding, or slow, presence. I thought it could be because I'm testing my personal subjectivity against the more objective qualities I can see in the group, a phenomenon I came across in the work of Donna Ladkin. This need to test the sense I'm making also comes from my need for approval, which for me results from not making mistakes.

While showing no presence 'Am I looking for a collective truth?' which in turn throws up further questions: 'Why am I looking for a collective truth?' Is it because I'm fully aware of my subjectivity or am I searching for others' truths to reach out to with my truth?' I felt in my bones that this was what I needed to look into – and I knew that I needed to do this in the company of others.

I started this informally, inquiring with my colleagues, curious about how they experienced me. In their eyes I was almost excellent in supporting others and showing presence. What I heard as I met with them in the follow up meetings was that they were learning how to show presence from me, and they get full support from me through my willingness to make personal disclosures of myself. Something was making me uncomfortable. I was disclosing so much of myself that I was forgetting to support others.

I was preparing an introductory presentation about myself and in that presentation, I put up a picture of a woman and a child, which expressed taking something and giving to the child which I described as a metaphor of being supportive.

One of my colleagues called this out as 'sacrifice' which upset me and pushed me to pay attention to my theme of 'supporting others' in another way. Who was I choosing to show presence to? What were the frames I was using to decide which relationships shaped the type of presence I was using? In some I preferred to show these qualities and there were some I preferred not to do so.

Discovering that I had frames and realities in my relationships, I was curious where and how these frames were formed and what they really meant for me? This curiosity pushed me to rethink my case and inquiry. There were many questions in my mind. All these questions were letting me think and reflect like a juggler, juggling the thoughts, questions and ideas to find my inquiry statement...

Like throwing balls in the air in juggling, throwing the thoughts, reflections, ideas, questions.... Sometimes it seems hectic! Sometimes anxiety comes and visits me, keen to see how long this back and forth will last!

It's messy, but when you get the joy of it, you like to practice again and again! At last you find how easily everything gets synchronized and you derive meaning!

## Resistance and Support

While working on my inquiry and my initial personal action research, I came across resistance and support co-existing together at the same time. The way I experienced resistance to my inquiry from some, and support from others, was significant in terms of my engagement with my colleagues and my dissertation.

From the first presentation I prepared I had a question in my mind 'Is this really my case?' Is it something I want to develop, work on to progress? Although I was very sure regarding the themes and topics during the journey of my Masters' thesis, I was seeking for approval from others who knew me. I decided to get a second opinion from my colleagues, as critical friends.

My colleague Ralf who knows me very well in a business context, asked me 'Why are you choosing to work on something you're doing well? Why are you asking how can you relate better? You believe that you're not relating well and are trying to find a solution to something which isn't a problem!'

I heard from another colleague, Lara, 'Do you really think you're not good at being relational! I learned being relational from you!' On top of these two another colleague, Alya, told me 'I do not think that this is your "case".' I was disappointed; even though I was seeking critical views, the feedback was painfully bringing me back to my starting point, which was not a progress.

The second resistance, resistance in me began to show itself. I felt like I was lost, endlessly seeking for approval. Not getting it made me question myself. I began to torture myself, desperately seeking for a new inquiry topic. I was ready to wipe away all the work and observations I'd made, just to have an inquiry statement which was welcomed by my colleagues. On top of this experience, I got together with my supervisor and my supervision group to review and give feedback on our dissertation drafts. After I'd shared my inquiry and my process I was asked: Who was I writing this dissertation for? The group urged me to look at my roots and link my inquiry to them – and then imagine the change I wanted to see in myself by the end of it. I was angry. I felt they were pushing me somewhere and whatever I said wasn't enough. I was unable to describe myself and finished the review in tears.

Afterwards Lara came and asked how I was feeling. I told her that I was really upset and asked 'Why are you pushing me? You are judgmental about me! You think I don't care about myself?'

At that moment, I saw her beautiful eyes looking at me, full of curiosity asking me 'Didem, I can't spare you; how can you do this to yourself?' I felt compassion, a warm compassion and asked myself 'How can you allow this to happen to you?' 'How can you forget yourself, your needs, your wants and instead try to please others and their desires?'

This was the turning point for me, to approach myself with the compassion that Lara reminded me to have. Even now, writing that question 'How can you allow this to happen to you?' It still feels like I'm torturing myself.

### *Journal Reflection:*

*My colleagues critical challenge of my inquiry statement made me silent at first but when it came up for the second time in our group meeting, I got very angry. I was tearful. I was like a 5-year old child who'd made a mistake and was being accused of what they have done. I was also angry with myself for feeling a failure. What was I missing? What is it that I'm not aware of and everyone is pushing to make me see? What does it mean to look at your roots? How can someone look at his/her roots? What will happen? I'm feeling squeezed, fearful and ambiguous. How can I say that my case is supporting others? I can't support myself yet. I just wanted to leave the room. I wanted to be with myself only. Then I heard my inner voice telling me I should stay and talk, not go. I stayed and even reflected with Ralf, which made me calm again.*

All these questions were with me for almost two weeks. I was full of thoughts flying in the air.

At that moment the bold question for me was 'What is the change you imagine for yourself?' And the bold statement that

Lara had said to me 'I can't spare you!' Now I decided to speak out about what I wanted, boldly, to myself and to others.

The change I imagine for myself is to exercise choice in my relations with others, saying NO to others if what they want doesn't support me. To tell myself that it is OK to accept my relational frames, be aware of them and then think about other options, and choices.

To live the relationships I'm in with liberty, without putting role, gender and approval frames on them.

To remind myself that there is no good or bad way to truly behave and to act what I believe in boldly with my presence. To seek and ask for my needs and wants. To change the focus to me rather than others.

## How Do I Relate as a Leader?
## My Second Cycle of Inquiry

In my first cycle, my relational frames coming from my family and life world became more obvious.

In my second cycle I decided to go to others to hear, reflect and learn about how I am relating with them. I decided to hear from a mixed group of people whom I had been interacting with and leading as a team in a community called Leaders Café. It was a group of volunteers working to design the theme and content of the annual Human Resources Conference held by the consultancy company I work for.

There were eight in the group, and I had a different relational dynamic with all of them. Five worked in leading Turkish organizations in different sectors and three were from my company, one of whom is my subordinate, so we have a hierarchically framed relationship while the other worked in a different team.

Leading this group is not something written into my working responsibilities or performance scorecard, but I believe that this process adds value to our Human Resources Conference which I co-chair. I feel I have a responsibility to support the Conference and the members of the team to get ready to share their experiences in their companies with the wider world. It was at the closure meeting we had, at the previous year's conference, when I asked if they could spend 15 minutes at the end of the meeting to support me. I sensed confusion and curiosity at the same time in their faces. During the meeting they were looking at the clock to leave enough time for me, which made me excited that they were excited and willing to support me.

### *Journal Reflection:*

*... There was confusion and curiosity among the group members. I know why, this is the first time I'd ever asked something for myself from them. This is very unusual for me, even with others who I'm in a relationship with. I was still very stingy with myself, in terms of asking for time from them... 15 minutes was a very small amount in a four hours workshop. I was trying to make them feel that I was not stealing their time for myself. I never thought this would also be a learning for them. I was shy to ask something from them....*

I set the scene by telling them about my inquiry into the support I needed. I asked their permission to record the conversation. I also told them that I did not want to hear positive feedback or their view on how good I am. I asked them to talk from their individual perspective and tell me about what kind of a relationship they experienced with me, when I was leading the group. I said that I would only listen and thank them. They started to speak spontaneously, with smiles on their faces. I felt their excitement as they waited their turn to speak to me, which I found encouraging. I felt supported at that moment.

I had questions in my mind about asking them to speak up, I'm aware that in our Turkish culture people are conservative when giving feedback or sharing their thoughts about someone. They would prefer to be complimentary. I did not take notes while the talked, I just looked into their eyes and welcomed what they had to say.

Here is what they said, and I have highlighted what I wanted to select for my inquiry.

**Helen, Human Resources Manager:** 'While working with this group I needed someone who would balance my positivity and negativity. Against my panic, my excitement, my 'Oh my god what am I going to do' style, **as a leader I got tremendous support from you.** Your cool style balanced me. At my panic moments your explanations relieved me. I felt that support. Also **sharing academic information** and gathering us, **when someone takes too much time politely making it run for all of us, or if someone does not speak, encouraging them to speak up showed me you were there with your presence. I wished you'd gathered all of us before the Conference and make us feel that you are with us.'**

**Sarah, Human Resources Director:** 'Regarding your presence; **the positive energy** while we enter the room, the liveliness and warm welcoming attracts me. Later you provide **valuable knowledge**, also you provide us with wise counsel. I do not know if you are aware of it or not, but you coach with your questions and you make me think more deeply. As **for your supporting behavior, whoever asks you something you try to support them**, once I asked for an article on culture even though you were on business trip - within 24 hours you'd provided me with the information I needed. I enjoyed your leadership; that's why I come from Ankara to Istanbul for our meetings. I see you always being calm, I also want to add something about the way you manage our time together, when someone takes responsibility for that they push people. When we come here, we sometimes haven't done the preparation we were supposed to have done. We start the meeting lacking in the belief that we can achieve what we need to get done. You relieve our fears and **encourage us and make us think that we can do it.** You do not push but you send the message that we need to pull ourselves together. There are many things to learn from you. I looked for you, **I wished you were with us in our presentations at the Conference.'**

**Monica, Human Resources Manager:** 'When I hear your name, three things come to my mind. Intimacy, trust and learning with counselling. When I met you for the first time, welcoming us to the workshops we did together, the one thing in my mind was intimacy. **I know that if I need any support in any topic, you'll be there to support us**; you did not tell us this, but you made us feel this. For the counselling, you did not tell us, but you made us tell ourselves, so with your guidance we spoke up. **I wished you were also with us during the presentation at the Conference.'**

**Mathew, Learning & Development Manager:** 'Your energy and communication are warm. Your energy never stops. You are not affected negatively. If you think differently you say so but always very politely. **You always make us feel good during these meetings**. This is also a part of it, asking us about yourself.'

**Malory, Adviser in a University:** 'Elegance is the word that comes to the surface. Your approach is graceful. In this gracefulness there is also the space you opened for our presences. You are calm, you are open. You share, you are open with your ideas and feelings. At first, I had doubts, I wondered whether this open, calm, elegant woman would be able to make sure we delivered the outcomes we needed. Then I saw how good you were with managing time during the meetings, never losing the focus on the target while also staying calm and open. **I also get inspired for myself by this.** Balance is something I see in you. **Knowledge and feelings are like a wave in the water; there are ups and downs, but they are always balanced. There are no extreme ups and downs. I saw and learned that calmness and openness can be in harmony. You were very tired one day; you shared this with us, and you delegated to one of your team members. By sharing and delegating, you encouraged that person.'**

**Paul, Project Consultant, Team member:** My experience is different with you. We are progressing together on a journey. This has two parts: the progress of our company and my own personal journey. I would describe your leadership as having depth. You look for something on the surface, but you can't find anything of note. If you look more deeply then you see many things. We are opposites! I'm trying to become like you, become calmer and deeper. I'm an extravert. I look for recognition from outside of myself and this is a very big challenge for me to work with in our business life. **But I learned many things, she contributes to my progress with silence. Sometimes I can't see at the surface but when I look inside, her presence, she is giving her hand to me; nourishment is there.** I'm now noticing that our differences are enjoyable! I enjoy your different leadership style, not screaming that you are leader and that I need to do something. Instead you make me think, question myself and take action accordingly. I'm used to this after all this time. You do something very provocative: you **push me from my inside; you push inside out as a leader.**

**Brianna, Marketing, working across functions:** I've experienced how you work and lead in these Leader's Café meetings, I was working with another leader in previous meetings. In them the events were not planned before. The group decided when and where to meet at that moment. You are different. Everything is planned when working with you and I was scared because I thought the group would not accept this. But later I saw that this was needed. You combine your blue analytical energy with enough yellow outgoing energy. You respond positively to all different points of view. **Even if you do not think in the same way, you never say 'No'. I never heard 'No' from you, there is always a way, a possibility.** One more thing, you delegate work and **you never stay around while the work gets done. But you always make us feel your presence** during that work. I feel your power behind me.

**Efe, Marketing, working across functions:** For me you are a very calm but also very strong leader. **You can be feminine and masculine at the same time when it is needed.** You have deep leadership; sometimes your glance is enough, your smile or your e-mail is enough. **You pass your message through your presence.**

*Journal Reflection:*

*… I felt very shy as they spoke. I knew that my face went red from the start. I'm noticing that it is not easy for me to listen to people talking about me. As my focus is always on the other,*

*looking at myself sitting in that hot seat, I was surprised how hard it was for me to listen to their thoughts about me. I was also torturing myself with my inner voice saying 'you asked in this way and they tell you good things dear lady'... ...*

When everyone had spoken in turn, I recognized that some wanted to add more because they'd been affected by the thoughts of others. It was like popcorn popping in the pan; flow was in the air and they were juggling me and my qualities when I was leading the group.

The thing I never thought, and was new for me, was that they also wanted this experience for themselves. They asked me to arrange a workshop so each of them could sit in this hot seat and get feedback as well as strokes from others. This was a new learning for me, as a leader, to put myself on the spot and make them experience it, be part of it and encourage them that they can do it too. I was not the leader of the group at that moment; socially we created a process that each time one of them took this role in the hot seat, whoever was talking, they were the leader. We had created a collective sense-making process which emerged from our web of relationships and generated knowledge for our group. This reminded me of Uhl Bien's work on Relational Leadership, which I'll speak to later.

What I see from the multitude of different theories and definitions is that academia can't come up with either a common definition or a shared framework for leadership. In my 23 years as a consultant, I have often heard about the differences between leadership and management. I'm still exposed to many different approaches emphasizing various frameworks like traits, behaviors, skills, or relational aspects of leadership. As Donna Ladkin (2010) says, leadership is a complex phenomenon and it tends to disappear as we try to look closer.

I would like to define what I mean by leadership and how it has changed since I started looking at it. During my career I've drawn on a number of frameworks. My relationship with theory shifted during my Masters' study and added a new way of looking which for me was quite challenging. Throughout my studies I found critical reflection very hard during written assignments and I ignored any theory or framework which did not resonate. I also had a tendency to focus on simple, ready to use, pragmatic, so-called scientific theories that would fit easily and satisfyingly into my practice. I found myself attracted to the work of John Kotter and his '8 Steps Change Process', Dave Ulrich's 'Ways to Create Leadership Brand' and Patrick Lencioni's 'Five Dysfunctions of a Team'. They all helped me to create easy to use—and easy to buy—development curriculums for my clients.

After reading the philosophers Edmund Husserl, Martin Heidegger and Jean-Paul Sartre, it became harder to take such works seriously. I liked a description of Edmund Husserl which Donna Ladkin brought to my attention in her 'Rethinking Leadership' book. She indicated that Husserl reminded the scientists of the time that all their laboratory-based formulations about the world, seen through abstract mathematical relationship and idealized circumstances (for instance, in worlds of flat surfaces and in which lines can extend forever) had limited application to the three-dimensional world of human beings. I treat this as a reminder crucial for my practice today.

During the last decade much has been written on the relational aspects of Leadership. Uhl Bien outlines two ways of studying leadership in the literature (Uhl Bien, 2006). The first she calls the entity perspective, which views leadership as an individual entity linked to traits and characteristics of leaders. The second perspective is the relational perspective which views leadership as a socially created process that can be embodied by an individual at any time.

Relational leadership asks how the processes of leadership and management in organizations emerges, how realities of leadership are interpreted within the network of relations. How organizations are designed, directed, controlled and developed on the bases of collectively generated knowledge about organizational realities. How decisions and actions are embedded in collective sense-making and attribution processes.

From a critical point of view, I'm pondering the question of what relational practice really brings to a leader and to an organization. How does this fit within the culture of Turkish organizations, does it really make sense?

Can leadership really be embodied by an individual at any time? Is it really like that or is leadership a nominated role which lasts for a period of time? How does the existing culture provide--or not--a space to lead relationally?

Relational leadership needs time to curate the socially constructed processes in small team settings and organizations. Experiencing directive leadership is a short-cut to getting things done.

Will organizations lose time and energy while experiencing Relational Leadership?

What I noticed from my second cycle of inquiry in terms of the relational qualities as a leader are that I'm:

- Using calmness and openness as a way of relating to others and generating encouragement for the other in the relationship.

- Using knowledge and information as a way of cultivating presence by using expert power and creating and sharing knowledge in relationship with others.
- Using the power of questions to increase awareness of the other, using polite language and creating a space for others to be present in the relationship.
- Using 'YES' rather than 'NO' to give a space for the relationship itself.
- Using any kind of connection to own my presence in a relationship and create dependency on me.

What was most significant for me in terms of my inquiry was Brianna telling me **'Even if she does not think in the same way, she never says 'No'. I never heard 'No' from her, there is always a way, a possibility.'** This was the moment I felt like shouting: Yes! I never say No, I learned to say YES to supporting others. Always thinking beyond myself for the sake of others or our relationship.

This was a pattern I used for my clients and in my family setting, I always find a way to fulfil others' needs and wants, to please them or to achieve an outcome. When you first hear this, it sounds as if this is something that supports the relationship, but it was not supporting me anymore. The way I participated in relationships made me disappear.

The second significant thing for me was how almost half of the group members wanted me to be with them more. Even when I'm on the stage chairing the conference, they want me to motivate them and encourage them for their presentations. I'm noticing that the more you give and give ease to the lives of others, the more the demands on you increase.

### *Trying to say 'NO' in Action*

I never worked on saying 'No' to people and I never knew that was what was going on. But why? I could see how patterns from my childhood, trying to adapt myself to get approval from my parents, especially my mother, were still alive and well in my adult behaviors. I was re-playing these ways of behaving that I had decided on as a child. The 'Adapted Child' part of my Child ego-state, to use the language of Transactional Analysis, still had a grip on me.

Eric Berne's transactional aspect is exactly what it says: a two-way communication, an exchange, a transaction. It supports a relational approach to life and leading. I remember a definition that TA supports: talk with the client rather than talk at the client, which became a motto for me when describing it. So how I talk with others was a discovery point for me in my inquiry and how I adapted myself to the world. I chose to say YES instead of NO.

My practice as a consultant also supported this behavior. As a consultant I always said YES to clients, giving them the impression that there is a way and I can support them in this way. Mostly this succeeded, but I needed to work hard all the time which exhausted me. This pattern also cascaded through my team, my subordinates. One day, one of the project consultants who had worked with me for two years had had enough and said to me: 'Didem, are you aware we as a team are working much longer hours than all the other teams.' I was aware that I demanded more than my colleagues, but now I also noticed that my unexamined habit of saying YES created more tasks and more responsibility for me and my team.

Social constructionist leadership approaches common-ly exhibit two interrelated characteristics. First, they eschew a leader-centric approach in which the leader's personality, style, and/or behavior are the primary (as in only) influence on their follower's thoughts and actions. When leaders are the pri-mary symbolizing agents, followers putatively surrender their right to make meanings by virtue of their employment contract with the organization (Fairhurst, 2001; Gronn, 2002; Smircich & Morgan, 1982).

Instead most constructionist leadership approaches place a premium on the ability of followers to also "make sense of and evaluate their organizational experiences" (Meindl, 1995, p. 332). The emphasis is given to leadership as a co-constructed reality, the processes and outcomes of interaction between and among social actors.

Communicative practices—talk, discourse, and other sym-bolic media—occasioned by the context are integral to the pro-cesses by which the social construction of leadership is brought about (Fairhurst, 2009).

As such, there is a resistance to essentializing theory in which leadership is to be found in a leader's personal quali-ties (e.g., trait theories), situational features (e.g., Hersey and Blanchard situational theory of leadership), or some combina-tion thereof (e.g., contingency theories such as when a crisis and strong leader coincides; Grint, 2000, 2005).

### Journal Reflection:

*... What would happen if I was to say NO rather than YES for myself? Is it right? Who knows what is right, why am I thinking that in that situation I need to say YES? Could I do it for the sake*

*of the other, by saying NO, I will also create a new possibility for the case. What would happen if they get disappointed if I say NO? This will create distance between the other and me. I will lose that relationship and maybe that opportunity. If this is a business issue, I'll be unable to get results and be seen as unsuccessful....*

I'm noticing that there were times when I said 'No' in the moment but later when I see this person being disappointed, I backtrack and want to find a way to make the situation better for them, give them what they want.

I decided to act and see what happened. To be on the safe side, and not take the risk of losing relationships and business, I decided to start at home. My daughter is 16 years old and hears a lot of NO from me. She's always trying to push the boundaries to get what she wants.

After my first NO to her, I always find myself doing something which, while not exactly what she wanted at that moment, is very close to what she wanted. I decided to focus on staying with my NO with her over a two-week period. I started by paying attention to how I said NO, saying it in a balanced way in the context of her needs and wants. She asked to go and play a game in her friend's house; she asked to play with her IPAD for more than the limited time she's allowed; she asked for new clothes; she said she needed to play with me. I consciously said NO to most of these requests.

During the second day of my research on saying NO to her, she told me that I had changed. I asked what she means when she said: 'Mummy, you are changed'. She told me that my face was not smiling, my voice was loud, she was experiencing me being more direct, angry and because of this she felt unhappy.

I was not surprised, this was exactly what I was expecting, my saying NO made others unhappy. And I notice that I still think about the other, not myself. I'm now encouraging myself to notice whether when I say NO, it gives me time to breath, feel relaxed and feel more spacious in my mind. Now to test if it really is like that? I decided to try to say NO in my work with clients. It was so hard, and painful. People who I've been working with for a long time don't expect me to say NO. It was so painful for me.

Following an organizational change, I became responsible for 20 key accounts in different industries. This meant I didn't have the time to dedicate to some of my existing clients. One of them was an international pharmaceutical company based in Turkey which I had been working with for 10 years. I needed to pass this client relationship and its projects to another team which was specially formed to work with this type of client.

The Human Resources Director of this company, who knows me and my work very well, wanted to go on working with me. I knew it would be hard to tell her that I wouldn't be able to deal with their projects anymore. I decided to invite her to lunch.

During the meal, as I was explaining our new business model, she suddenly asked me 'Are you saying that it will not be possible to work with you?' She went on: 'If you do not work with us, we won't be able to do projects with your company anymore.'

At that moment, I felt the same feeling of being squeezed, squeezed in a box and wanting to hide in the middle of nowhere, but I couldn't. I couldn't say NO. Instead I said: 'I'll find a way to work with you.' My trial was unsuccessful, I could not take the risk of saying NO. Losing a relationship or piece of business was unbearable for me. It was like losing a very good friend forever. Unable to say NO to this client cost me a lot. I needed to leave my friends after my dissertation and immediately return to work for this client. No time to celebrate with them. I didn't see my daughter for two more nights. I needed to do more meetings, prepare presentations and spend time on them.

The result is we retained the client and they will continue to work with us. The other gained again.

*Journal Reflection:*

*… …Should I describe this story as a win lose game? Is this a game with myself? I only tried…*

## My Learning

I'm noticing a pattern after all the cycles. Each time there is a good intent in me to get a job, to start a relationship, to envision a project which excites me, where I can see the end result and its impact on my progress. Then I begin to visualize it, assume my responsibilities, prepare others, try and work hard, long hours to reach that result. Then it becomes bigger and bigger, tasks become bigger, responsibilities get bigger. I begin to feel tired, exhausted and as I look after others, I believe that either they are not aligned with me or not working as hard as me for that result. I get angry and start to blame myself, sometimes blaming others as the cause of my tiredness.

When I blame others, I feel guilty and squeezed. I choose to leave the situation or relationship; if I can't leave, I put distance between the situation and me or in my relationship with the other. I separate from the situation or relationship and reflect. It makes me even more tired.

After this deep tiredness I remember what my father said to me: 'We have one life.' I remember my responsibility to my family, my company and, without making any changes, I think I've healed myself and come back to the same situation and relationship. I visualize this round trip like this;

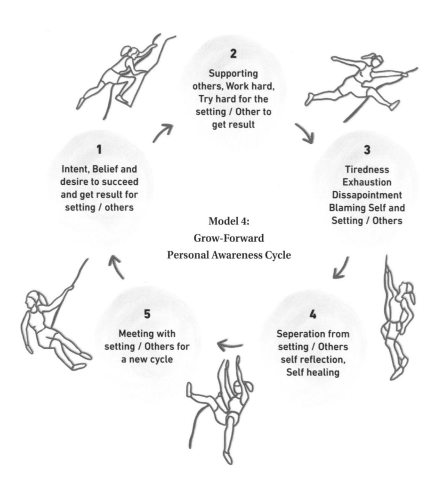

**2**
Supporting
others, Work hard,
Try hard for the
setting / Other to
get result

**1**
Intent, Belief and
desire to succeed
and get result for
setting / others

**3**
Tiredness
Exhaustion
Dissapointment
Blaming Self and
Setting / Others

Model 4:
Grow-Forward
Personal Awareness Cycle

**5**
Meeting with
setting / Others for
a new cycle

**4**
Seperation from
setting / Others
self reflection,
Self healing

As I'm aware of this cycle now, I'm asking myself 'What are my choices in this cycle to support myself? What other qualities do I have that can support me to overcome this cycle more easily?'

## Grow-Forward for Myself

### *Describing the Shift*

In my inquiry, I described the transformation I dreamed of as 'The change I imagine for myself is to live my relationships with others by exercising choice and saying NO if it will support me. To tell myself that it is OK, to accept my relational frames and think of what other options and choices are available to me and then decide which to use with this deeper awareness. To live my relationships with liberty without putting role, gender and approval frames around them. To remind myself that there is no good or bad and truly act on what I believe in, boldly and with presence. To understand my needs and wants and ask for them to be met. To change the focus onto me rather than always on others. To find a way of supporting myself! To find a way of expressing my needs and wants...'

Looking forward encourages me. I also like getting power from what and how I have acted in the past. This co-existence of looking forward and backwards reminds me of a beautiful mythical bird called Sankofa.

The word SANKOFA is derived from the words SAN (return), KO (go), FA (look, seek and take). This symbolizes the Akan's quest for knowledge with the implication that the quest is based on critical examination, and intelligent and patient investigation.

The Sankofa bird flies forward with its head turned backwards, reflecting the Akan belief that the past serves as a guide in planning the future and that by learning from the past we build the future.

The Sankofa Bird looks backwards with the egg of the future in her beak, constantly checking as she moves into the future...

## Actions

| Team Vision | Team Reflection | Hard Work Dedication | Constructive Interaction |

## Skillset

| Alignment | Team Leadership | Decision Making | Collaboration |

## Mindset

| We share common purpose | We are whole with our diversity | We can co-create together | We can do |

Model 2: Grow-Forward Delta Model
Team, showing three layers of Grow

CHAPTER FIVE

## GROW CIRCLE IN THE SENSE OF TEAMS AND ORGANIZATION

### Action Research, A Grow Women Leadership Circle

I mostly work with teams which are formed by organizations and have a clear purpose, and most of the time the problems, patterns and scenarios they face are very similar and familiar.

While working on Grow, I had a desire to work with a group whose purpose is to Grow. With this in mind, I created an inquiry statement, 'In a group setting can learning and growing through sharing knowledge and experiences lead to a change in our lives or not?' I decided to start a Grow Women Leadership Circle.

I believe when a woman supports another woman, they both benefit. When women celebrate one another's accomplishments, we're all lifted up. Together, women can do more, go further, and facilitate greater change in the world. As a personal mission, I wanted to support women leaders who are new in their management roles. Drawing inspiration from Sheryl Sandberg's 'Lean-in Circles', I dreamed of starting a GROW Circle with a group of women as they set about developing themselves as people and as leaders of teams and organizations.

So, I wrote and sent an invitation letter to eight Companies, from a range of sectors, and asked each of them to nominate a woman who had a similar background to me. All the companies nominated a participant and so we began, with one other woman coming from my own company.

## My Invitation to Companies to Nominate a GROW Women

A GROW Woman's Circle is a small group of eight women. They meet regularly on the last Thursday of the month. The group supports one another to develop as leaders, to work through actual situations and learn new skills.

The Participants' Profile for joining the Circle are:

- √ She has more than 5 years of experience in organizational settings.
- √ She is in a management role and managing more than three people.
- √ She is eager to learn and progress in her career.
- √ She has grown-up and been educated in a small town and then moved to a big city.

### *The Grow Topics will cover:*

- √ Growing the sense of self
- √ Growing the understanding of woman as leader
- √ Growing the capacity for achievement

There's power in belonging to Grow Circles. They are places where we, as women, can give voice to our dreams and find the encouragement to start pursuing them. They're a place for sharing ideas, gaining skills, seeking advice, and experiencing connection and solidarity. Most of all, they're a place where we help each other become our very best selves. They're a place where we learn to reach out into the wider world and not just focus on our own lives and those of our organizations. As part of the development process, each woman in the group will be expected to make a Grow Action that will impact the greater society in their organizational setting or in social life.

And it starts with your organization making a nomination. Who is the woman in your organization who needs the support of other women to thrive in her career? Who could make much more of a contribution to your organization if she had the support of other women on the same journey? The Grow Circle is what will deliver what she and you both need.

## Grow Women Leadership Circle in Action

I thought I needed to contact each participant with an initial personal touch. I wrote a welcoming e-mail indicating my purpose and intention. I also gave space for them to share their thoughts about how we were going to work, where we'd meet and what our timing would be.

Each of them sent me some thoughts about how their purpose linked with this Circle and what they would like to transform.

My intention from the start had been to experiment with how to grow in a different type of team setting; now the par-

**Growing the sense of self:**
Definition of GROW Growth Mindset, Skillset and Actions
GROW: Self Discovery and Planning

GROW Circle Intention, Principles Harvesting Our Circle Story
Crafting a Personal Brand Values Excercise

**Self Paced**

**Reading
Watching
Visiting**

**Growing the sense of woman as leader:**
Leading as a Woman Defining your S Curve and Self Mastery
GROW: Leading with Relational Power

Defining Personal S Curve Leading with Relational Power in Change
Ways of Knowing as a Women Centered Presence Exercise

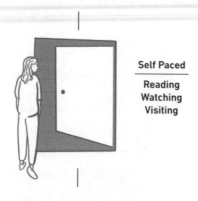

**Self Paced**

**Reading
Watching
Visiting**

**Growing the sense of achievement:**
Leading with Impact Leading Challenges - Case Lab
GROW: Leading with Positive Impact

Leadership Challenges Courageous Conversations
Your Splash, Social Impact Influence & Impact Excercise

**Model 5: Grow Circle Action Group Development Structure**

ticipants of the team were sharing their expectations for themselves as well as the group. They seemed very open and willing to participate but I also sensed curiosity about how it was going to transpire, and who the other members of the team were.

I was also excited and anxious. Somehow their expectations created a sense of responsibility in me and I started to prepare our first gathering. I know the first gathering is always a defining moment for the orientation of a group. I created a structure and suggested topics to work on. I was aiming to get their contributions and finalize this before our face-to-face gathering. On the day, I was ready with my pre-prepared, crafted flipcharts and ready to tell my story and to listen to theirs.

## The Face to Face Gatherings

Our first gathering was an amazing occasion to witness Grow in action. Nearly everybody arrived on time, one was late, and one didn't show up. Everyone was on their own and nobody spoke that much with each other. There was a lot of eye contact, people observing each other.

I welcomed everyone with good music and my flipcharts. My main objective was to create a sense of belonging and trust. I knew that this comes from the facilitator and I was aware that how I showed up really mattered. I needed to model desirable behaviors like openness, curiosity, listening, encouragement and sharing expert knowledge on the topics we'd cover. I thought that would be enough.

After making a social contract which I titled 'Our Grow Manifesto,' we set about gathering the guiding principles which would serve the group. I used the term Manifesto because its much bolder than a team contract statement. We went through each of our guiding principles and committed to act on them in our gatherings.

Our Manifesto has 10 statements and each statement indicates commitment to the Circle;

*Our intention is to grow*

*We believe in the power of circles*

*We share responsibility for our circle outcomes*

*We listen to each other with curiosity and compassion without judgement*

*Any personal material shared is confidential*

*We ask for what we need and offer what we can*

*We are here & now, supporting each other, knowing that the circle needs us*

*We rotate leadership*

*We find opportunities to practice what we have learned*

*We always allow ourselves time for reflection*

I introduced an exercise for people to tell their life story through. It was a process I knew and trusted and was based on the idea that since we are human, we are storytellers. Often the stories we live by are so deep we don't even know that they are running the show, but they always show themselves!

I went first and then asked for volunteers to follow. We were in the flow of things. Each story made us go deep into this person and their persona and connect with them. Some stories were very similar; some were hard to believe. In the end, what struck us was the richness of the stories and commonalities, as well as the group connection that had been developed through their telling.

By the last story, I noticed how our circle had moved physically closer together, with everybody leaning into its center. None of us was the same person--we weren't the same group as we'd been at the beginning. I saw, sensed, felt the progress. Grow in the air.

Each gathering started with a check-in process in which we connected with our personal and group thoughts and feelings as well as what we were bringing to the Circle on that day. Each gathering had its closing ritual which allowed us to experience the power of reflection, learning and Grow. And if we experienced anything which was not fitting with our Manifesto, we had the right to speak up.

Creating a personal brand was another area we focused on during our gatherings. We used all the data we had from our lives, knowledge of our strengths, our defining moments and the qualities that had supported us in the ups and downs of our lives over the years.

Then with the structure in 'Five Steps to Building Your Personal Leadership Brand' article (Dave Ulrich and Norm Smallwood, HBR, 2007), I encouraged us all to create and share our own personal brands. I went first, showing my personal brand:

> 'I want to be known for being enthusiastically integrative, for bringing clarity with pragmatism and for being persistently decisive so I can become the most preferred and recommended Organizational Development and Management Consultancy company in Turkey and the near far east.'

I chose leadership qualities like Decisive, Persistent, Integrative, Clarity, Enthusiastic, Pragmatic for myself and asked them to form four qualities from their strengths and two qualities from the development areas they wanted to progress in the next 12 months. They all believed this was important, with one participant sharing this personal reality: 'I always thought it was important but never tried to make one for myself.' After she shared this, I saw nodding heads and supporting voices. I gave enough time to work on it, did not push them to the result, and we agreed to talk and give feedback/feedforward to our personal brands to support each other.

As we agreed to have virtual gatherings at our first meeting, virtual call platform supported us as a collaboration tool to get together. We all agreed that the quality and depth of participation was as great as in the face-to-face gatherings. We were curious about this and on reflection we all agreed that the self-interest, getting responsibility to grow, doing something for ourselves made it much more focused.

I also invited speakers from outside the Circle to join us, to share different perspectives and learning from other disciplines. One of the most popular sessions was the business etiquette and presence session. I once again learned how some topics are very common for women and we have a shared need to talk and discuss them. I was observing a lively and vibrant feminine energy in the air.

## Grow for the Team and Me

As a Grow facilitator, I see the shift from the first gathering in a new team. There is a process that you need to put in place which is:

- A strong why, and engaging the why with the team, with personal purposes
- Crafting a structure of topics to be covered and the process to be in place
- Creating trust and harmony in your style, getting commitment
- Shift facilitation leadership in the team
- Involve them, address challenges
- Reflect and boldly frame the new learning

Key learnings sharing from the team;

- I needed this; it's my time to be in this Circle and support myself
- I'm sharing my new learnings with my team and supporting them in their Grow Journey
- The feedback I have heard in this group makes me think about my preferences and how I create a context to transform them
- A-ha moments--now I understand why I'm thinking in this way, how it affects others.
- I learned how to appreciate others in this circle

I observed the power of belonging to Grow Circles. The Circle was a place where we as women gave voice to our challenges, dreams and found the encouragement to start acting on them. We encouraged each other and will continue to do so...

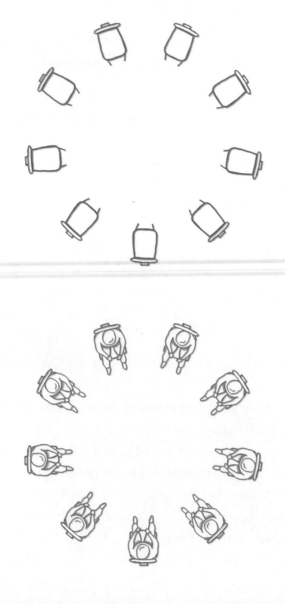

## GROW-FORWARD MANIFESTO FOR
## FINDING YOUR NEXT STEP

I believe in circles. Symbolically, the circle represents completeness, wholeness, unity, oneness, strength, and original perfection. I describe my Grow-Forward journey as one where I have invisible circles around me.

Each time I seek out for a stretching, new experience, I see that I'm going beyond the boundaries of the invisible circles that I have been confined within. Then I can easily make moves into the space of the bigger circle. If I don't make a move, then I'm squeezed into a very small circle which traps me. It's important to go beyond your comfort zone and make change and grow possibilities for yourself, by testing and going beyond the edge of your circles.

If you know where you are, are full of insight and want to step up for yourself, you need to describe your delta for who could you be. What's the motto for your Grow? Who would you like to be in your career and life journey? It's worth taking responsibility to work on your future more than anything else in your life, because it's your one life.

*GROW-Forward Manifesto*

*I can grow and shape a better me in every moment*

*I take accountability to be conscious of
who am I and my impact on others*

*I proactively craft my Grow-Forward plan for the future*

*I value myself and explore every opportunity
to Grow-Forward*

*I value people around me, their insights about
me and I seek their support*

*I value others to listen, share and
Grow-Forward together*

*I feed my curiosity and am alive with
experimentation in this world to Grow-Forward*

*I learn from my failures, I feel the pain and
mobilize my inner willpower*

*I listen to my mind, body and soul to
find the way to Grow-Forward*

*I appreciate my Grow*

# ENDNOTES

1. Carol Dweck, Mindset

2. Robert A. Nisbet, History of Progress

3. McNiff & Whitehead, Doing and Writing Action Research

4. Joyce K. Fletcher, Disappearing Acts: Gender, Power and Relational Practice at Work

5. Bruce Tuckman, Forming, Storming, Norming and Performing: Successful Communication in Groups and Teams

6. William Isaacs, Dialogue and The Art of Thinking Together

7. David Whyte, The House of Belonging

8. Michael M. Lombardo, Robert W. Eichinger, FYI For Teams: Based on the Team Architect, for Team Members, Team Leaders, and Team Coaches

9. James Clear, Atomic Habits: An Easy & Proven Way to Build Good Habits & Break Bad Ones

10. Eric Berne, Transactional Analysis in Psychotherapy: A Systematic Individual and Social Psychiatry

11. Claude Steiner, Emotional Literacy

12. Donna Ladkin, Rethinking Leadership: A New Look at Old Leadership Questions

13. Uhl Bien, Advancing Relational Leadership Research: A Dialogue among Perspectives (Leadership Horizons)

14. Dave Ulrich, Norm Smallwood, Leadership Brand: Developing Customer-Focused Leaders to Drive Performance and Build Lasting Value

15. Gail T. Fairhurst, The Power of Framing: Creating the Language of Leadership

16. Peter Gronn, The New Work of Educational Leaders

17. Linda Smircich, Critical Perspectives on Organization and Management Theory

18. James R. Meindl, Follower-Centered Perspectives on Leadership

19. Hersey and Blanchard, Management of Organizational Behavior

20. Keith Grint, Organizational Leadership

21. John Kotter, Leading Change

22. Patrick Lencioni, The Five Dysfunctions of a Team: A Leadership Fable

23. Mary Tolbert and Jonno Hanafin, Use of Self in OD Consulting